Witnesses of a Third Way

Witnesses
of a Third Way:
A Fresh Look at
Evangelism

Henry J. Schmidt, Editor

BRETHREN PRESS
Elgin, Illinois

WITNESSES OF A THIRD WAY:
A Fresh Look at Evangelism

Cover design by Kathy Kline

Library of Congress Cataloging-in-Publication Data

Witnesses of a third way.

    Material drawn from the plenary sessions and workshops of Alive '85, held in Denver, Colo., Apr. 11-14, 1985.
    Bibliography: p.
    1. Evangelistic work — Congresses. 2. Anabaptists — Congresses. I. Schmidt, Henry J., 1940-
II. Alive '85 (1985 : Denver, Colo.)
BV3755.W57   1986   266'.97   85-27981
ISBN 0-87178-940-X

Printed in the United States of America

Contents

List of Contributors

Arthur Climenhaga, Resource Ministries: Evangelism, Bible Conferences, Missions, and Seminary Professor-at-large; Mechanicsburg, Pennsylvania.

Myron S. Augsburger, Pastor of the Washington Community Fellowship and former Moderator of the Mennonite Church, Washington, D.C.

David Ewert, President and Professor of New Testament at the Mennonite Brethren Bible College, Winnipeg, Manitoba.

James Myer, Bible Conference speaker and former Moderator of the Church of the Brethren, Lititz, Pennsylvania.

Robert Neff, General Secretary of the Church of the Brethren, Elgin, Illinois.

Frank Tillapaugh, Conference Speaker and Senior Pastor of the Bear Valley Baptist Church, Denver, Colorado.

Henry Ginder, Messiah College Minister at Large and Spiritual Life Speaker with the Brethren in Christ, Mechanicsburg, Pennsylvania.

John Neufeld, President of the Canadian Mennonite Bible College, Winnipeg, Manitoba.

Palmer Becker, Pastor of the Peace Mennonite Church, Vancouver, British Columbia.

Arthur G. McPhee, Evangelism Seminar Leader and Church Planter, Boston, Massachusetts.

Don Jacobs, Executive Director of Mennonite Christian Leadership Foundation, Landisville, Pennsylvania.

Christine Michael, Staff for Urban Ministry for the Church of the Brethren General Board, Elgin, Illinois.

Henry J. Schmidt, Associate Professor of World Mission and Director of Mission Training Center at the Mennonite Brethren Biblical Seminary, Moderator of United States Mennonite Brethren Conference, Fresno, California.

Donald E. Yoder, Secretary for Church Planting and Evangelism, Mennonite Board of Missions and General Conference Mennonite Church, Tempe, Arizona.

Preface

At the 1974 International Congress on World Evangelization in Lausanne, Switzerland, one representative from a newer Mennonite community in Europe looked at a gathering of North American Anabaptists and said, "As new members of this Anabaptist fellowship, we have been studying diligently the historic roots of our heritage. We read concerning our Mennonite and Swiss Brethren fathers and mothers that they went everywhere chattering the Word. But we do not see you doing that in North America. What has happened?

Naturally we were glad to be able to report on the evangelism value of PROBE '72, an Anabaptist evangelism consultation held in Minneapolis, Minnesota in April, 1972. In addition to that conference we cited the strategy of planting new congregations and modest church growth as evidence of our continuing concern in North America for evangelistic outreach. And yet some of us also had to confess that our brothers and sisters had put their finger on a continuing deficiency.

Since then, we have had concerns regarding our peace witness, the implications of justice and social concern, our position toward government on such issues as taxation, class distinctions and allied matters. But through it all and especially in the Council of Moderators and Secretaries of the Mennonites and Brethren in Christ, we were drawn in a spirit of renewal back to primary questions of evangelism. During my chairmanship of the Council of Moderators and Secretaries, we began to plan for a major event focusing on evangelism. The event became known as Alive '85. Others in the Anabaptist family joined in as well, the Church of the Brethren and the Brethren Church (Ashland). Groups such as the Missionary Church and Mennonite churches not in the Council of Moderators and Secretaries also had representatives at some planning meetings and at the Alive '85 itself.

Alive '85 took place April 11 to 14, 1985 in Denver, Colorado. The convocation of approximately 1,500 people was an inspiring

event. The program brought in a wide range of evangelism expertise both in plenary addresses and workshops. As presentations
have been readied for publication they have been prepared to give a
systematic presentation of the conference's theme and message. Dr.
Henry J. Schmidt, professor at Mennonite Brethren Biblical Seminary in Fresno and vice-chairman of the Planning Committee, has
been largely responsible for accomplishing this task.

The two-section arrangement covers the content and context
involved in sharing Third Way Anabaptist evangelism. In the first
section following Myron Augsburger's definition of churches of the
Third Way, three scripturally-based presentations speak to biblical
models for evangelism along with a discussion of the church as a
covenant community. All four presentations are made by persons
who are or have been pastors, administrators, moderators, and
who are representative leaders of three of the major denominational groups involved in ALIVE . . . '85. The fifth chapter comes
from a guest speaker of a fraternal Baptist community challenging
Anabaptists to innovative methods in unleashing the church community for ministry in the Third Way. Concluding the section is a
presentation by a long-term church pastor, leader, bishop emeritus,
and continuing evangelist speaking to the place of the Holy Spirit in
empowering the people of God in performance of evangelism
ministry.

The second section begins with the primary consideration of
conversion moving then into the urgent necessity for discipling of
new converts. The persons speaking to these areas are successful
pastors who have also been administrators or teachers. Chapters
which follow deal with several areas of evangelism in a fresh way:
lifestyle; peace, evangelism and social justice; urban evangelism vision and strategies. These writers also are or have been pastors,
teachers, evangelists, and in one case, an overseas missionary with
training in anthropology. The concluding chapter issues a challenge
to multiply churches in the Third Way, presented by one who is
carrying out such multiplication.

These chapters are not written by theorists but by men and
women who have tested and proved what they have written or
spoken in the crucible of daily experience. These concepts are
working in the lives and practice of peoples and churches in the
Third Way. Therefore, this book should be an excellent tool for
elective Sunday School classes on a quarterly basis, for mid-week

studies, home Bible studies, or church training institutes. A sense of direction is evident in this work to help us move forward in evangelism and church planning endeavors in the 1980s and 1990s. The people of God known as the Anabaptists once again have caught fire "to go everywhere chattering the Word" and building covenant communities of God's people today.

Arthur M. Climenhaga
Chairman, Alive . . . '85 Program Committee
Former Bishop and General Secretary,
Brethren in Christ Church

Introduction

Alive '85 brought 1500 pastors, church leaders, educators and lay persons to Denver in a four-day Evangelism and Church Growth Consultation. The participants represented seven Anabaptist denominations: Mennonite, Church of the Brethren, General Conference Mennonite, Brethren in Christ, Missionary Church, Brethren Church and Mennonite Brethren. These denominations have a common history, arising out of the reformation movements of the sixteenth and seventeenth centuries. In addition to a strong emphasis on personal conversion, discipleship, believer's baptism, the free church and membership in a visible community of believers, Churches of the Third Way have a strong commitment to mission. Telling the good news to neighbors and friends has been a concern — whether fleeing persecution or going about our daily work.

The term "Churches of the Third Way" describes the Anabaptist commitment to Jesus Christ as "the way, the truth and life." It is intended to portray a stripe of the evangelical church that is committed to radical biblicism and discipleship. Such a commitment places Anabaptists in a mediating position within evangelicalism because we are not easily classified as: extreme left or right, pietist or modernist, nationalist or anti-government, conservative or liberal, flaming evangelists or social activists. Commitment to the Lordship of Jesus Christ means that our primary concern is to be an obedient, faithful church, that seeks "first the Kingdom of God and his righteousness." Such a position frees us to move beyond labels, categories, and stereotypes to identify with both sides on particular issues while maintaining an unswerving commitment to Jesus Christ as Lord. It also means we risk being misread and misunderstood on some issues because we prioritize "obedience and faithfulness to Jesus Christ" over pragmatics and alignment with mainline cultural values.

The material included in this book has drawn from the 12 plenary sessions and several of the 85 workshops offered at Alive

'85. The stated purpose of Alive '85 was to celebrate the good news of Jesus Christ, to share what God is doing among his people, to examine the meaning of faithful evangelism in the midst of a variety of evangelistic voices, and to worship the God and Father of our Lord Jesus Christ. The purpose of this book is to reflect the agenda and perspective of Churches of the Third Way at the close of the twentieth century. It addresses the relevant topics of biblical church models, the meaning of church and of a ministry mindset, the role of the Holy Spirit in evangelism, conversion and discipling issues, peace, justice and social concerns, friendship evangelism, a vision and strategies for urban evangelism, and church planting. The book, which includes 13 chapters with a study guide and bibliography, is deliberately designed for more in depth discussion as a Sunday School elective or mid-week study group.

As editor, I owe a debt of gratitude to many people who have helped to make the dream of some permanent record of Alive '85 become reality. In addition to the chapter contributors, I thank the Alive '85 Editorial Committee consisting of Arthur Climenhaga, Myron Augsburger, Floyd Bartel and Paul Mundey for their helpful suggestions in editing the manuscript. The untiring editorial and secretarial work of Peggy McAlister, Kent Gaston, Ruthanne Willems and Debbie Wright at the Seminary is deeply appreciated. It has been a privilege to work with David Eller, book editor at Brethren Press. My prayer is that this book will bring a Third Way perspective that helps churches fulfill their ministry of "reaching the lost" and "maturing the saints."

Henry J. Schmidt
Fresno, California

1

Churches of the Third Way

Myron Augsburger

Evangelism always begins with God's initiative. God in His grace has come to us and called us to life in Christ. We are sinners who have been saved by His grace. We did not make the first move toward God. It was God who came to us and called us. "For God so loved the world that he gave His only begotten Son that whosoever believeth in Him should not perish but have everlasting life" (John 3:16).

It is important for the various Mennonite and Brethren denominations to be reminded that we are not in the Kingdom of God because of our history or heritage. We are in the Kingdom of God because of the transforming grace of God in Jesus Christ. The same is true on a more personal level. None of us is involved in evangelism because of our perfection, achievements and successes. The only reason any person can bear witness is because of the grace of God. We who stand in the Anabaptist heritage of the Christian church with a strong commitment on mission and evangelism cannot overemphasize the grace of God.

There are many people in the world who are doing evangelism. Some Christians and some non-Christians are doing evangelism for their movement. Within the Christian church, evangelism is being done in a variety of ways. Some methods are good and we applaud them. Others are an embarrassment because they are not befitting the gospel of Jesus.

As evangelical Anabaptists our understanding of Jesus shapes our evangelism methodology. We believe the ways we evangelize must be appropriate to the context of the people and cultures with which we work and share. Our evangelism is not because of some legalistic constraint, but it springs from the joy of knowing Jesus Christ. In fact, evangelism can be defined as anything and everything that makes faith in Jesus a possibility. Evangelism is simply being a channel through which God meets people and invites

them into His fellowship. We are proclaimers of the good news —
not good views but good news. And that good news is that you may
become a child of God. This is God's offer of grace.

Churches of the Third Way — The Way in Jesus Christ

The topic "Churches of the Third Way," suggests that there are
different approaches to evangelism because of the particular stance
of some evangelical churches that are not working in the same way
some others do. This is not to critique or belittle other groups.
Jesus needs to be lifted higher in every church. In addressing this
theme, the focus is an understanding of what evangelism means for
churches of the Third Way.

What does it mean to be churches of the Third Way? In Col.
3:10-11, Paul writes of this life created in Christ Jesus, "there is
neither Greek or Jew, circumcision or uncircumcision, Barbarian,
Scythian, bond or free." In another passage he adds, "there is
neither male nor female, but all have become one in Jesus Christ."
In today's vocabulary our designations would be different. We
would say, in Christ there is neither east nor west, northern
hemisphere nor southern hemisphere, First World nor Third
World. There is a new way in Jesus Christ that is neither mystical
nor merely rationalistic religion. There is neither total ideological
commitment nor full cultural affinity. There is neither nationalistic
identifications nor revolutionary involvements. There is neither
parochial literalism nor synergistic humanism. But there is in Jesus
Christ something other that lets us speak to all of these without
becoming enslaved to any one of them.

The Book of Acts presents the disciples of Jesus Christ as being
followers of the Way. We are not calling people to a philosophy or a
culture, but to a Person. If our Christianity is more identification
with an ethnic pattern or a tradition than it is with the disclosure of
God in Jesus Christ, then we have missed the heart of the gospel.
And in doing so, we cannot be evangelistic. If we have turned to a
kind of legalism that perpetuates a religious tradition, even with
high ethics, but fails to understand the dynamic of the Holy Spirit,
who transforms people's lives, we will not be evangelistic. It is not
the efforts that we are involved in that change people's lives. It is
rather that we witness to the fact of meeting Him, that He by His
Spirit transforms people and brings them into the Way.

There is no Christian culture to which we invite people, nor by which we judge people. Neither is there a kind of socio-political stance by which we critique everyone. For example, when we moved into Washington D.C. to start a new church we said we are neither rightist conservatives nor leftist secularists. We are followers of the Third Way, the way of the Kingdom of Jesus Christ. That allows us to see benefits that we can select from these other dimensions. It allows us to be involved as persons who can be prophetic in relation to them. But it means that we are always seeking to witness to the fact that the new life is the life in Christ.

This means then that we discover anew that Jesus came introducing another way. In short, it is the way of the Kingdom. The way of the rule of God. The way which he called the Kingdom. But in saying this we must remember that there is no Kingdom without a King. And you have not adequately talked about the King unless you talk about his kingdom. I say this because I do not want in any way to be misunderstood as though I would champion a Kingdom without the Christ. To do so would make one guilty of the plagiarism that borrows nice things from Jesus and goes out to build a kingdom, without admitting that unless people meet the King, they are not going to become a part of his kingdom.

On the other hand, I do not want to talk about the king and divorce him from the reality of his rule in people's lives now. One cannot separate Jesus from the actuality of a kingdom in the present. For it was this Jesus who clearly taught that there is a kingdom. The way to get into it is to be born a second time by the Spirit. (John 3) It was this Jesus who said, "I give you a kingdom as my father has given me a kingdom" (Luke 22:29). And it was a disciple of this Jesus, the Apostle Paul, who said, "God has translated us from the kingdom of darkness into the kingdom of his dear son." Paul declared in Acts 20:28, "I have gone about among you declaring the gospel of the kingdom of God." And again as Paul wrote to the Romans, his message was "this kingdom of God is not little rules about meat and drink, but righteousness and peace and joy in the Holy Ghost." Paul reminds us that the perspective of churches of the Third Way, is the Kingdom. It is a fellowship of people who are committed to the King and to his way.

There is in American society a myth that needs to be exploded. It is a myth that if one has a conservative theology, one must also have a conservative political and social view. The very fact that one has a conservative theology, which includes: belief in the inspiration of Scripture, as an infallible rule for faith and practice; belief that Jesus is actually the Son of God, that he died and rose again, that he lives, and that he has a kingdom, etc.—the very fact that one takes all of these beliefs seriously means that one can be very free and selective in terms of the other kingdoms of this world. One can decide when and where support will be given to earthly movements because one speaks from the perspective of having pledged ultimate commitment to the King and to his kingdom.

Jesus Christ is building a kingdom. That kingdom is not to be identified with any cultural or national position. Some people have sought to see the kingdom of God in America and almost equated the kingdom of God with Americanism. However, the kingdom of God stands confronting America with a call to a spiritual awakening and renewal. Other people who think that to be a part of the kingdom of God means to be anti-American, need to be reminded that such a position also violates the nature of the Incarnation. Jesus could walk among Jewish persons and yet minister to the hated Roman centurion. He did not bring castigation upon either group. By his actions he challenged the Jewish people to recognize that the way of the kingdom is a way of peace and love for those who are your enemies. To the Roman centurion, Jesus' ministry as a Jew to a Gentile was a powerful reminder that the kingdom he proclaimed was not bound to an identity with the Jewish community.

The Challenge For Churches of the Third Way

The challenge facing Anabaptist evangelicals is to model this commitment to a third way. Churches of the Third Way build a fellowship that can reach across the boundaries that humans create. Sometimes those boundaries are, in their simpler forms, cultural. Other times they may be, in religious forms, denominational forms. Or again, they may be, in nationalistic forms, lines between nations. But the Christian church needs to model before the powers of the world the fact that people that are from various nations, races, and cultures, can be one fellowship in Jesus Christ. As churches model this reconciliation, some of the powers that are perplexed about how to change relationships might begin looking to us as an example that associations can be different. The energies of

quence of the witnesses, in the power of persuasion, but in the Spirit of God.

To say that the Word came with "full conviction" may be a reference to the deep conviction which the apostles had, that their gospel was indeed the power of God unto salvation. And unless we have this deep conviction we will hardly have the courage or strength to carry on our witness. However, it probably includes also the deep conviction the hearers had, that what they were hearing was indeed the word of truth on which they could stake their lives.

We cannot fully explain the operation of the Holy Spirit in empowering God's message any more than we can grasp how electricity charges a bare cable with high voltage power; but we have plenty of evidence for it. This awareness that only the Spirit of God can convince the hearer of the truthfulness and authenticity of the gospel, makes the one who proclaims the gospel very dependent on God. Spurgeon was often overheard as he walked to his pulpit in his tabernacle in London, mumbling to himself, "I believe in the Holy Spirit, I believe in the Holy Spirit."

This message was strengthened by the exemplary lives of the messengers: "You know what kind of people we were for your sake." In some disciplines of learning it may not matter very much what a person does in private. I had a brilliant professor of chemistry at the university, but he drank quite heavily. In the Christian ministry, however, our witness lacks authenticity if our life does not jibe with our teaching. What helped to convince the Thessalonians of the trustworthiness of the gospel was the kind of life the apostles lived. It was lifestyle evangelism.

Paul moves from eternity into time — the coming of the gospel to the Thessalonians; but then he draws the circle even narrower, and speaks of the personal response of the hearers to the gospel. "For you received the word in much affliction with joy inspired by the Holy Spirit." "To receive the word" is another way of saying that they believed or obeyed the gospel. "Faith in the New Testament sense," as Oscar Cullmann puts it, "is the way the past phase of redemption becomes effective for me." They welcomed the word.

And there was nothing superficial about this decision. "You became imitators of us and of the Lord." They became *mimetai* — mimickers. Not literally of course. John Wiens, missionary to India, limped, and he claimed all his converts also limped. We must not forget that these early converts had no New Testament and they had no Christian traditions to follow. How then should they live? By imitating the Christian life of the apostles! And lest Paul should appear to sound presumptuous he quickly adds "and of the Lord." As if to say, what they imitated in Paul was what he had learned from the Lord; they followed the Lord by imitating the apostles.

Further evidence that their faith commitment was deep and strong was the fact that they were willing to suffer for the sake of their faith. They endured "tribulation," and these trials did not quench their holy joy, for it was inspired by the Holy Spirit. So often in the New Testament suffering and joy stand side by side and that should remind us that Christian joy is not euphoria, laughter and giggles. It is that deep peace that comes from the assurance that we belong to God and that he is leading us to glory. It is eschatological joy.

Practical Expressions of the New Way of Life

"So that you became an example to all the believers in Macedonia and in Achaia." The faith of these converts cut deeply into their lives. They began to live in a new way. And Paul commends them for their Christian deportment by saying that they became *tupoi*—types, models, examples, to other believers. There is a commentary on the epistle of James written by Guy King, which has the title "A Faith that Behaves." And that is still the best evidence of the new life in Christ.

Not only did their new faith affect their feet (i.e., their daily life), but also their mouth. They had something new to say. "For not only has the word of the Lord sounded forth from you in Macedonia and Achaia, but your faith in God has gone forth everywhere, so that we need not say anything."

From you sounded forth (*exechetai*—used only here in the New Testament means a loud ringing sound) suggests a trumpet call. From the city the gospel was taken to the surrounding countryside. There is no suggestion here that all the Thessalonians became itinerant evangelists, but neither can it be inferred that none left Thessalonica. Thessalonica was a throbbing metropolis and we have here another example of Pauline strategy—to plant lighthouses at the crossroads of culture.

But once he established a Christian community it was left to the local congregation to carry the gospel further. And they did. And this should certainly be the pattern for us today. The missionary concern of the church and its efforts to reach others with the gospel is a sign of the vitality of the church. "Your faith has gone everywhere," says Paul—a forgivable hyperbole.

"And how you turned to God from idols to serve a living and true God." This is what conversion meant for gentiles in the first century: to turn from idols to God. And that means more than switching from polytheism to monotheism in one's thinking. It went deeper than that. They turned from serving idols to serving the true and living God.

The question may be asked: How does this apply to the western world? We may never have worshiped idols. What must we be converted from? Perhaps we should not be too quick to give up this language as irrelevant. Martin Luther once defined idolatry in this way: "Whatever your heart clings to, and relies upon, that is properly your God."

Do not the gods of ancient Greece and Rome appear repeatedly in new dress? Mars in the militarism of our day; Minerva in our worship of the intellect; Vulcan, the ironmonger, in our craving for technological achievements and gadgetry; Venus in the sex-emphasis of our society. We need what Thomas Chalmers of Scotland in a memorable sermon called "The Expulsive Power of a New Affection." Unless we are clear in our understanding of conversion our mission efforts will be greatly hampered.

In the last verse of this chapter Paul strikes a note that will become more and more pervasive as he moves along in his Thessalonian correspondence: the return of our Lord. Paul thanks God that his converts had turned their eyes to the future and that they lived their life in the hope of the return of Christ. They "waited for his Son from heaven."

The object of the waiting is the Son. The eschatology of the New Testament is overshadowed by a person, the person of Jesus Christ. Not events, not a calendar of apocalyptic happenings, but a person stands in the center of the Christian hope. "We wait for the Savior from heaven."

The basis for this hope is the resurrection of Jesus Christ. Because he rose triumphantly from the grave and ascended in great majesty to heaven, he will come again. Karl Heim, German theologian and scientist, compared Christ's resurrection to a small crack in a dyke in Holland. To begin with there was only a trickle, but eventually the North Sea poured into the Lowlands. Christ's resurrection was a crack in the vast prison house, death, and all those united with him follow him, when God's hour strikes, into an endless life with God.

This glorious appearing of Jesus Christ does not frighten the believer; for the one we wait for "delivers us from the coming wrath." And that strikes a solemn note. Without the conviction that in the end all humankind must stand before God's judgment throne, our missionary task will be greatly weakened. God's wrath is already revealed from heaven in the judgments of history, in the hardening of people's hearts when they reject the gospel, and in other ways. But Paul thinks here of that final judgment of God upon all those who reject the good news of salvation.

This wrath is being held back at the moment by the patience of God, for he wants all people to repent. For us as believers, who have the blessed hope of Christ's return, the great commission stands as a permanent challenge to go into all the world to make disciples. And if we do, we have the assurance that Christ will be with us to the end of the age.

The impact of the Thessalonian church on the surrounding areas of Achai and Asia Minor obviously has its roots in a solid theological orientation. As people of the Third Way they knew that their "work of faith, labor of love and endurance of hope" was anchored in the choice of God's love, the power of the Gospel and their obedient response of faith. The results of their commitment demonstrated itself with unmistakable clarity in a new deportment, communication, devotion and expectation. The Thessalonians became a "sounding board" for the gospel and a "sending agency" in terms of multiplying their witness in their world. The challenge facing churches of the Third Way today is to model the integration of faith and works; God's initiative and man's obedience; healthy congregational nurture and strong evangelistic zeal; turning from idols and serving the true God.

Questions and Ideas for Discussion

1. If you were asked to identify a follower of Christ today, what would you look for?

2. As you understand the New Testament, what kinds of

works would you expect a person with a living faith to produce?

3. What practical significance does the doctrine of election have for you?

4. How would you define Christ joy?

5. Can you suggest ways in which believers can share their faith with others today?

6. How were you converted "from idols" to serve the living and true God?

3

Biblical Characteristics of Third Way People

James F. Myer

John 17 is one of the greatest prayers of Jesus Christ for the church. It is really the Lord's Prayer for His people. It is much more the Lord's prayer than the one we usually call the Lord's Prayer, which is more of a disciple's prayer. John 17 gives one a clear sense of Jesus' heartbeat in his prayer for the church today. No passage in scripture gives us a better picture of the present intercessory ministry of Jesus in his concern for the character and mission of His people in the world.

In the first 12 chapters of John's gospel, Christ is presented to the whole world. In chapters 13 to 23 he is presented more in relationship to his own followers. For example, in John 13 Jesus washed the disciples' feet as a symbol of servanthood and cleansing. In John 14, Jesus promised a prepared place for a prepared people. In the 15th chapter Jesus is presented as the living vine who sustains and nurtures his disciples. And in the 16th chapter Jesus promised the gift of the Holy Spirit to encourage, strengthen and comfort his people. In John 17, Christ's prayer is for the church — for people of the Third Way. He reminds his disciples that God is in the business of drawing out of the world a people.

The primary job of God's people is to cooperate with the Holy Spirit in that process. It is God who draws people out of the world, but he does it through his redeemed people in the world. At least seven times in this prayer the expression occurs, "those whom you have given me." It is a reassuring reminder as we engage in evangelistic activity, that whenever we faithfully share the gospel message, God is already at work in the hearts of people who are being called to accept the message of salvation.

John 17 has some powerful, subtle strategies for the kind of evangelism Jesus wants churches of the Third Way to perform. The thrust of this chapter is not to rush out into the world and to corral a multitude of people. It is not to hustle them into the kingdom with every method that will insure large numbers of noses, and nickels. It is another kind of evangelism. The focus here is on how to get the church to really be the church. The emphasis is on quality body life within the family of God, so that as the church moves out in evangelism, it has a strong base of quality within the body of Christ upon which the base of evangelism activity can be built.

There are many essential gospel principles in this prayer that are important to remember in the church's evangelist activity. There are eight marks of distinction that Jesus places upon churches of the Third Way in this prayer which include: 1. the scope of new authority (v. 2); 2. The development of a new relationship (v. 3); 3. The formation of a new understanding (v. 8); 4. The reality of a new protection (vv. 11–12); 5. The experience of a new joy (v. 13); 6. The call to a new holiness (v. 15); 7. The challenge of a new outreach (vv. 18–21); 8. The winsomeness of a new unity (v. 21).

The Mark of God's People

The first mark of God's people is the scope of a new authority. The prayer begins with an acknowledgement of Christ's authority over all people (v. 2). One of our tasks in evangelism is simply to announce to the world that Jesus Christ is Lord over all people. We are not out on our own auspices. At the close of Matthew's gospel Jesus says, "All power, all authority, is given unto me in Heaven and unto earth." (Matt. 28:18). During Jesus' earthly ministry there were people who commented that "He taught as one who had authority." (Matt. 7:29) He even reminded Pilot, in those tense moments prior to the crucifixion, "You could have no power against me except that which were given you from above (John 19:11). "Even in those delicate situations Christ did not forget the scope of authority that God had given to him. Some people commented about his miracle performing power, "What manner of man is this that even the wind and sea obey him?" (Mark 4:41) At Jesus' temptation it is a bit amusing that Satan was so bold as to suggest to Jesus that if he would bow down and worship him he would give him all the kingdoms of the world. (Matt. 4:8–9) What would Satan have done if Jesus would have said "it's a deal"? Satan would have discovered that Jesus was a difficult one to relate to because Jesus has ultimate authority. Christ's scope of authority becomes ours in the church. We are on earth to do business with all people in Christ's name, that is the scope of our new authority.

A second distinction of Third Way people is the development of a new relationship. Verse 3 defines what eternal life is all about, "Now this is eternal life that they may know you, the only true God in Jesus Christ whom you have sent." This is a reminder that we are to develop an intimate knowledge of Almighty God. An intimate knowledge of Jesus Christ is Christ's way of saying we need to develop a new relationship. The Greek word here for *know* goes beyond mere intellectual knowledge. It includes the idea of seeing and understanding as well as experiencing the true God.

There are a great number of gods for the world to see, know and experience today. For example, Paul encountered them in Athens in Acts 17: "Men of Athens," Paul says, "I see that in every way you are very religious, for as I walked around and observed your objects of worship, I even found an alter with this inscription, 'to an unknown God.' Now what you worship is something unknown, I am going to proclaim to you (vv. 22–23)." If we were to display the gods of this world, we'd need a much larger arena than they had on Mars Hill. But the challenge is the same, to notice that among all the gods there is really only one God and there is only one Jesus Christ to whom we give our allegiance in a new relationship.

It is this call to spiritual intimacy that Jesus is praying for in John 17. "This is eternal life, to know the only true God. And Jesus Christ whom you have sent." Paul had a lot of religion in his life. But he came to the place where he said "I count all these things as loss that I may know Christ . . . that I may know him and the power of his resurrection" (Phil. 3:8–10). It is one thing to know about Jesus, it is another thing to know Jesus, personally and experientially. Jesus' invitation in Revelation 3:20 is still the starting point for all of us. "Behold I stand at the door and knock. If any man will hear my voice and open the door, I will come in to him and will sup with him and he with me."

A third mark is the formation of a new understanding. "For I gave them the words you gave me and they accepted them, they knew with certainty that I came from you and they believe that you sent me" (John 17:8). The scripture reminds us that the carnal mind is enmity against God (Rom. 8:7). It is a place of darkness. It is very obvious from the scripture that a new mindset is needed. In fact, the scripture challenges us to "let this mind be in you which was also in Christ Jesus" (Phil. 2:5). We must be bearers of the words of life. We must repeat "sing them over again to me, wonderful words of life." Our words must agree with the Words which we have been given by God. Actually our task is not so much a challenge to originality, as it is a challenge to faithfully share the words which we have been given just as Jesus shared the words which he had been given. Those words of life are found in the Bible and we need to go on record that God's Word is very important for us, and we are not ashamed to share that Word with the world. It is indeed in this message of Scripture that we have the clearest revelation of God's Word to the world.

One of the greatest challenges facing the church is to remain faithful to the message of Scripture. It is so easy to begin to tinker with it, to change it a little bit, and to try to make it fit the age so that it is less offensive. One of our greatest challenges as preachers is to remain satisfied with the basic message of God's Word and not alter it. It is like the lady whose husband passed away. After the funeral she wanted to have an oil portrait made of his face. So she took a snapshot to the photographer and asked if he could make an oil portrait. But she informed the photographer that there were a few things she would like to change if she could. She said, "You notice he has a little wart beside his nose, I want you could take that off. Also I'd like you to curl his mustache a little bit. He had such beautiful curly hair, paint him with his hat off so it will show his beautiful hair." The photographer was a bit puzzled, "Well, which side of his head did he part his hair?" She replied, "You know, I've forgotten but you'll see once you take his hat off." It is so easy to try to tinker around and make little changes.

Jesus is calling us to the formation of a new understanding. Recently, a person made an inquiry of me regarding my impression of a mission society that was involved in translating the Bible into another language. As we exchanged our perspectives on that work, the other person concluded the conversation by saying, "I believe it is a good ministry if you believe it is important to get the words of the Bible into the minds of people." There is no room for "if" in that statement. The assumption is that getting God's word to people is a priority agenda. Jesus said, "I gave them the words you gave me and they accepted them. They knew with certainty that I came from you and they believed that you sent me."

Reality, Experience, and Call

The fourth quality of God's people is the reality of a new protection. John 17:11–12 promises tremendous protection to the church. In those verses one can feel the arms of Jesus reaching around his children. One can sense that inner circle of Peter, James and John being expanded to reach around every true believer. Sometimes Anabaptist evangelicals are too hesitant to use the word "predestination." In our haste not to be identified with any extremes, we have failed to realize that a part of God's saving activity in the world is calling people out of the world, and keeping them in the church. None of us would make it if it were not for the saving redemptive activity of God in the world. He calls and keeps. In fact, it is not easy to fall away. If one falls away as a Christian, one has to determine to stumble over a lot of barriers that God has placed in one's way to keep one in the kingdom. There is protection promised here. The good shepherd of Psalm 23 and John 10 is an effective shepherd.

Jesus says a fifth mark of His church is the experience of the new joy. "I am coming to you now but I say these things while I am still in the world so that they may have the full measure of my joy within them." (v. 13) Christianity is something to be enjoyed. Following Jesus ought to keep us smiling and happy. Christianity is to be enjoyed, not endured. In that sense, it is like a good marriage. Too many marriages are an endurance test rather than a joyful adventure. It reminds me of that husband and wife who had not spoken to each other in three days. The wife noticed her husband was getting ready to take a trip and since they were not talking she just decided to get ready and go with him. When they were on the way the husband noticed some long faced donkeys in the pasture and for the first time in three days he broke the silence with a question, "Are you related to those animals?" She was ready for him. She replied, "Yes, through marriage."

How is it that some of our Anabaptist forebearers endured hardship and persecution the way they did? The testimony that comes from our history and from their mouths is that they lived with an inner joyfulness that carried them on in spite of the difficulties of their society. No wonder Jesus said, "My peace I give unto you. And I do it that your joy might be full."

A call to a new holiness is a sixth distinguishing mark of the people of the Third Way. Jesus prays not that his disciples be taken out of the world, but for their protection from the evil one (v. 15). Over the years Anabaptist evangelicals have said we are, "in the world but not of the world." Separation does not mean isolation, strange as it might sound in the modern age, but we are to understand the world as a hostile force. Satan is a real enemy. There is a battle being waged between the Kingdom of darkness and the Kingdom of light. There is a call to live by different values and standards as disciples of Jesus Christ. In our passion to reach the world we dare not fall prey to the same trap of many Christian groups, namely that bit by bit, piece by piece, inch by inch, the evangelical church has become more aculturated, more secularized, because it wants to be more respectable.

The identity that we are the people of God is always linked to a new call to holiness. There was a need for 16th century Anabaptist renewal movement because the larger church had become so worldly. Sometimes I wonder if perhaps God will need to bring a second Anabaptist renewal movement to rescue the first one. Our Anabaptist heritage had holy living as an essential part of its emphasis on discipleship and certainly that focus needs to be recaptured among 20th century Mennonite and Brethren Churches.

A New Outreach and a New Unity

A seventh mark of the true church is the challenge of a new outreach. "As you sent me into the world, I have sent them into the world" (John 17:18). The world is not supposed to penetrate the church, but the church is supposed to penetrate the world. God's people function like flashlights, punching holes in the darkness. There is a "go" in the gospel, that has been lost in much of the present day church. It is a "go" not just to people like us, or to where the good land is or to where the life is good. There is a "go" in the gospel that is ingrained in the New Testament.

One of the reasons we have had so much difficulty in recent decades in evangelism is simply because we have lost the urgency of the "go" in the gospel. Instead we expect that if we build a nice church building, if we announce our meetings, that the people will come to the church. This fact came home vividly to me just a few years ago when my home congregation built a new meetinghouse. It is large, and I am embarrassed to say how much it cost. But within less than a mile from where that big building was built, one day we were visiting door to door in the neighborhood. I introduced myself as one of the ministers from this new church that had been built in the community. The church was within easy sight of where I was standing on the front porch of a neighbor lady and she asked, "What new church building?" I thought to myself, "Impossible. Here we spent all this energy and money on a building and those within sight of it did not even know it existed." Is it possible that through television and other media abilities people know more what is going on on the other side of the world than what is going on next door? The church has to break down some of its formality if we are going to "go" into the world.

As moderator of the Church of the Brethren I visit a lot of congregations and have some idea why some Church of the Brethren congregations are not growing. I've been in some churches where I thought I was preaching at Mt. Rushmore. All I could see were the great stone faces. Everything is stiff, cold, formal. Those churches are dying, and they will continue to die. The challenge is for a new outreach. Perhaps our churches are like the man who was a great fisherman. After a thunderstorm he was seen fishing from his front porch in a mudpuddle. Somebody asked him, "Do you expect to catch any fish there?" He said "No, but it sure is a handy place to fish."

This prayer suggests that there is a winsomeness that comes from a new unity. One of the evangelistic principles from God's perspective is how the presently evangelized people on earth get along. I do not hear many people in the Anabaptist tradition bragging about how well we have done in that area. The winsomeness of a new unity, "that all of them may be one, Father, just as you are in me and I am in you. May they also be in us so that the world may believe that you have sent me" (v. 21). This is not a unity that is built on compromise. It is a unity that is built on integrity. It is a unity that is found in the unity of the Godhead. Jesus is saying, just as you and I have been one so the believers are to be one with each other. Just as this unity was seen in Christ's willingness to do the Father's will, it will be seen again in our obedience to the great commandments "to love the Lord your God with all your heart, with all your soul, mind and strength and to love your neighbors as yourselves" (Mark 12:30–31). In fact, Jesus said, on these two points hang all the law and the prophets.

Some great evangelistic principles are nestled in this wonderful prayer of Jesus. The starting point is not methodology or technique, but it is the quality of relationships among the people of the Third Way. God's starting point is not the world, but the church. When the church is renewed, alive and vibrant its message cannot be kept a secret. Jesus' prayer in John 17 challenges the church to develop quality relationships through a personal encounter with Christ which in turn will manifest themselves in a new authority, interrelationship, understanding, perfection, joy, holiness, outreach and unity.

Questions and Ideas for Discussion

1. John 17 focuses the primary of three relationships — a relationship with God, with believers in the church and with people in the world. Discuss the importance of keeping these three dimensions in balance in both personal and church life. What are the consequences of imbalance in any one area?

2. What is the relationship between the believer's authority and a sense of urgency in evangelism?

3. Why does Jesus stress the importance of unity among God's people as a basis for effective evangelism in the world?

4. Discuss the meaning of the phrase "in the world, but not of the world." What are some of the ways in which the church has become aculturated and secularized?

5. Jesus emphasized the challenge of a new outreach (John 17:18-21). How will a faithful church be marked by both qualitative and quantitative growth?

4

Church as Covenant Community in the Third Way

Robert Neff

If you were to name the greatest evangelist of all time, who would that be? A Graham, a Moody, a Sunday, a Finney, a Whitfield, a Wesley, a Fox? For me, the greatest evangelist of all time was the Apostle Paul. Paul was able to express the gospel and proclaim the faith all over the Middle Eastern world. Often he did it under considerable duress. He, probably more than any other individual, was responsible for the inclusion of diverse peoples within the life of the church.

If Paul was the greatest evangelist in the history of the church, what was the secret of his success? What makes him the evangelist that he was? I know the Anabaptist detractors on the sidelines are saying, "Here we are, trying to work at evangelism in the twenty-first century, and immediately you betray your Anabaptist heritage because you say everything significant happened in the first century. You go right back to Paul to talk about evangelism." But that is our departure point, that is where we do have clarity, and where we do find our bearings for what we are about as people of the Third Way.

While one cannot call Paul's conversion the only paradigm for Christian faith, it does provide one model of the conversion process and the church's role as a covenant community. Acts 9:1-19 provides a basis for understanding the evangelistic activity of Paul. Paul had been religious imperialist. He believed he was doing the very will of God in arresting Christians. He was certain in his own mind that this was what God wanted. He pursued the direction which had been set out for him. And is it not remarkable that someone so convinced, so absolutely sure, so firm in his conviction, listens to these words: "Saul, Saul, why do you persecute me?"

"Who are you, Lord?" A person dedicated to the will of God,

a person convinced that he is carrying out the will of God, cries out, "I don't know you; who are you?" "I'm Jesus, the Christ," came the vocal response. Religious imperialism blinded him. Religious fanaticism made Paul short sighted. The power of God is the power to stop Paul dead in his tracks.

C.S. Lewis in his autobiographical book, *Surprised by Joy*, says that we can talk religiously about God, for there is no danger of God's doing anything to us. [1] We have God securely in our hip pocket and therefore we couldn't possibly change. The power of God in Saul's life is to stop him dead in his tracks. God says "No" to a religious imperialism which pretends that "God is on my side and I can determine exactly what God wants me to do."

A Conversion Decision Takes Time

James Dunn, in his book *Baptism in the Holy Spirit*, says that for Paul to assimilate God's "No" took time. [2] This was no shallow experience. For someone to be so uprooted, so stopped, so challenged, took unbelievable time. Saul's blindness is an indication of the deep searching of the soul. It was a symptom of the shaking of the foundations which called for the re-examination of every assumption in Paul's life. Therefore, he remained in darkness, disoriented. He is caused to examine all the suppositions that have defined his life. Therefore, he sat for three days in blindness.

A good Anabaptist view of conversion, one that encouraged the thinking of Alexander Mack, is found in Luke 14:28: "If you go to build a tower, calculate what it's going to cost, calculate what it's going to mean, calculate that so the world doesn't scoff at you after you begin to build and are unable to finish it." Paul's conversion takes place over a period of time.

Some say, "Strike while the iron is hot." Set the context right, orchestrate the music correctly, create the right atmosphere. Then when there is a quick decision, that is sound evangelism. "But, which of us here, having a son or daughter who comes home and says, "I've found the most beautiful person in the world. I want to get married tomorrow," would say, "Strike while the iron is hot. How about making that choice tonight?"

A decision for Christ takes time. Even early church tradition says that it could have been three years in which that examination process took place. But that conversion is only the beginning. The subject of discussion in this chapter is life in the covenant community. Saul's conversion is not complete with that light-blinding experience. It is completed with the appearance of a man by the name of Ananias. Ananias is a person who has every right to be frightened out of his wits. He knew that Saul is in the area to serve a death warrant. It is then no wonder that only Ananias' prayer life and the mercy and power of God can direct him to the room of Saul. When Ananias shows up there, his words are simple. He does not deliver a sermon. One sentence carries the entire message: "Brother Saul, the Lord who appeared to you on the road has brought me here so that you may regain your sight and receive the Holy Spirit."

Healing, Acceptance, Serving in the Covenant Community

The completing of Saul's conversion is centered on three moments. The first is healing. To be in touch with the covenant community, represented by Ananias, is to receive healing, physical sight, mental reorientation, spiritual wholeness. To experience the Body of Christ is to receive full wholeness — physical, mental and spiritual.

The second movement in this drama is what Henri Nouwen refers to as "the shift from hostility to hospitality."[3] From murderer Saul to Brother. Brother! In that word is freedom. It is saying, "Through the power of God, I receive you as brother." There is a change from hostility to hospitality. That change is at the very heart of the gospel. One of the chief beauties of a personal testimony I heard today came in the words, "I forgive; I receive you as brother." No long evangelistic address, but only two words "Brother Saul." A move from enemy to guest. "I receive you as friend; I love you in the name of God."

Only the love of God could bring such love. And in talking about that, Nouwen says that we ought to treat one another somewhat like a flower. Our tasks in evangelism are to clear away the weeds, to pull away the rocks, to allow the plant to grow.[4] That is the tenderness of evangelism. Myron Augsburger has accurately said, "There cannot be a separation of peace from evangelism." At the heart of evangelism is the proclamation of peace, of wholeness, of oneness. That is what Paul's becoming part of the covenant community means. Ananias is there as a representative of a community.

He invites Paul to participate.

If one reads on in the Book of Acts, after the baptism and the receiving of the Holy Spirit (which means inclusion within the Body of Christ) is the nurturing time spent with the disciples. A person who had been caught in despair is now a person whose whole readjustment in life is included in the Body of Christ, sustained in the Body of Christ, healed in the Body of Christ. The scripture text states, ". . . he met with the disciples for a few days." Then what happened? Paul is out preaching! And later, as this scripture story reflects, he realized the importance of a support community. That same body of believers is the group who dropped Paul over the wall, assisting him in his escape. The conversion of Paul is a recognition that one belongs to a covenant community, a fellowship of believers. To know Christ is to know that the hostility is ended. One who was once an enemy is now a friend. That is demonstrated by the person who extends a hand and says, "God loves you, and you are now part of the fellowship."

An evaluation of the Pauline letters and his sermons is most revealing. It is striking that the greatest evangelist of all times left no collection of sermons except, the brief reports in the book of Acts. What we have is a commentary on Paul's priorities. The greatest evangelist has left the church with a series of letters that are about one thing: the building and sustaining of the Body of Christ. His primary concern was that there be a whole and vital Christian community. This is Paul's legacy to the larger church, a healthy concern for the people of God and a covenant community.

Paul talks about his encounter with Christ on the Damascus road. He talks about the resurrection experience, particularly when his authority is at stake, not unlike any other apostle who lived during the time of Jesus' earthly ministry. Paul says, "I, too, have had the authoritative experience, but what is important for me is to live in Christ." The key words for Paul are to live in Christ. Paul is saying, "I want Christ to permeate my life." Pauline Christology is not first and foremost lofty statements about Christ. The Christology of Paul calls people to personal and corporate commitment, "To what extent is Christ permeating my being? To what extent is Christ expressed in my speaking, in my hearing, in my knowing and understanding, and in my loving?" That is the power of Paul's witness.

Paul's repeated concern is with those who could misunderstand the faith as simply their own personal possession. When he wrote to the people at Corinth he said, "Now listen, just because you're carried away" (as one translation puts it), "just because you've had an emotional experience, that doesn't make you a Christian. Why any of the heathen could say, 'We've had an emotional experience too." Juvenale could say that the Orontes is flowing into the Tiber because eastern mysticism was the guiding religious force of the day. Paul says, "No, it is important to be moved, it is important to be empowered by that Christ, but, unless you find yourself in the Body of Christ, faith leads nowhere."

So the parallel chapters of Romans 12 and 1 Corinthians 12 talk about the movement of the Christian into the Body of Christ so that one's gifts might be released for totality of the Body. Fed by his experience from Ananias, it is Paul's understanding that one's experiencing of Christ is intended to bring us into a living relationship with one another. That is what it means to belong in the covenant community.

Paul constantly reminds us that we no longer look at one another from a human point of view. We are now new creatures in Christ. We bear testimony to the reconciling ministry of Jesus Christ. We are ambassadors for Christ. And in doing that, we find our place within the covenant community. We find ourselves in the Body of Christ.

In 1 Thessalonians, we find this beautiful verse that describes Paul's ministry: "We were gentle among you, like a nurse taking care of her children, . . . we were ready to share with you not only the gospel of God but also our own selves . . . " Paul's penchant for the church is the united body, Gentile and Jew, male and female, circumcised and uncircumcised. Paul says that to discover the power of Jesus Christ is to live at one within the Body of Christ. That's the evangelistic fervor of Paul; that's where he spent his life. His passion, his joy, was to see in the Body of Christ the spirit of the risen Lord. His desire is that when others see the Body they will see only Christ. That's the power of Pauline evangelism. That is what Paul is struggling to write to the churches. When we encounter Paul, whether it is tent-making with one group, visiting synagogues with another, or spending time with others, it is for one purpose alone: to know that when we experience the risen Lord, we are together in a healing community, that we embody that risen Lord by a life that we share together.

Implications for the Covenant Community Today

What does that mean for individual believers in the local church? What does this mean for the church as a covenant community today? John Naisbitt, in his book *Megatrends*, sketches out major themes for our society. One chapter entitled, "High Tech, High Touch," has particular application for the church.[5] Even though society is technologically advanced, there is still a need for honest and caring relationships. The need for the personal touch will continue to grow. That is the nature of our society. Every church growth leader will tell you that the most powerful force in evangelism is a healthy, vital church. A church that embodies the power and vitality of Jesus Christ will always be relevant.

Wayne Oates, the famed pastoral counselor, used to take his students to a neurologist in downtown New York. On one particular occasion, as the neurologist pointed to various brains that were in jars in the back of the room, brains that had been destroyed by trauma, arteriosclerosis, or lead poisoning, he said that there is one clue to a healthy, growing mind. That is a healthy, vital community. And Oates said, "After I returned home I thought of 1 Corinthians 12, and the nourishment that we find in that community." Without a nurturing community, no matter how many evangelistic services we hold, we will not hold persons. Without the support of a covenant community, new converts will struggle individually in no-man's land with little hope for maturity.

My earliest summer pastorate was in Virginia. About four years ago, a person who knew of my continuing interest in their congregation wrote, "We are doing great things in this church. We're going to fill the church. When we fill the church I'm going to stand on the roof and preach a sermon." About six weeks later I got the front page of a newspaper, "Preacher preaching from the roof tops"—a front-page spread. Five weeks later I got another letter. "It didn't work. We forgot something. We forgot something very, very vital—a nurturing, caring community. We were so energized for that big day that we forgot what bringing people into the church was all about, a vital Christian life together."

One Sunday morning I was in First Church in Chicago, and it was one of those mornings when the tenor didn't get out of bed on the right side. It was one of those mornings when you hear someone beginning to sing and you want to put your head between your knees. You'd just like to duck away, you'd like to forget the whole incident. As I listened to this faltering voice, I looked around. People were pulling out hymnals to locate the hymn being sung by the soloist. By the second verse the congregation had joined the soloist in the hymn. And by the third verse, the tenor was beginning to find the range. And by the fourth verse it was beautiful. And on the fifth verse the congregation was absolutely silent, and the tenor sang the most beautiful solo of his life. That is life in the body of Christ, enabling one another to sing the tune Christ has given us. It also is the voice of evangelism which sings the gentle tune of invitation to life in a whole community under Christ.

The greatness of Paul's life as an evangelist, church planter, theologian and missionary statesman cannot be accounted for apart from his relationship to the Church as a covenant community. Romans 16 is only one illustration of the list of people that Paul enumerates as colleagues and supporters in ministry, for which he thanks God. The drag of human nature and the trend of Western culture moves people down the pathway of increased individualism. The challenge facing churches of the Third Way is to invite people to deal with their independence and individualism in commitment to Jesus Christ in the context of the church. To say "yes" to Jesus but "no" to his covenant people is both parodoxical and unbiblical. The Lordship of Christ means little if there is no connection or accountability to His people. This is not to assume that the church is ever all it should be. But it is to say that we place a high premium on covenant commitment to fellow believers to be mutually taught, nurtured, discipled and strengthened.

Questions and Ideas for Discussion

1. What is the place of the community in announcing the good news of Jesus Christ?

2. How do you understand personal conversion as a communal event?

3. What are the marks of conversion?

4. Outline the steps of transformation in Saul's/Paul's life in Acts 9.

5. Think about your own conversion. What was the content and circumstance that led to this decision?

6. In what ways did the decision for Christ require a negation of past and cultural norms for Paul? For you personally?

5

Unleashing People for Ministry in the Third Way

Frank Tillapaugh

The church's ministry in the world can be hung on three pegs. Pegs number one and two are worship and edification (the church's ministry to itself). My primary area of concern, however, is the third peg — the church and its mission and impact on its environment.

Numbers 13:25-33 provides the backdrop for the subject of unleashing people for ministry in churches of the Third Way. The children of Israel are poised on the edge of the promised land. Spies have been sent in, and the Israelites await their reports. The minority report of Caleb and Joshua was optimistic. "We should go up and take possession of the land, for we can certainly do it" (Numbers 13:30). The report of the negative majority is recorded in Numbers 13:31-33. "We cannot attack those people. They are stronger than we are. And they spread among the Israelites a bad report about the land they explored . . . . And all the people we saw there are of great size . . . . we seemed like grasshoppers in our own eyes, and we look the same to them."

Numbers 13 is full of excitement. Hundreds of years before, God had promised Moses a land where he would build a nation. That nation was to be the heart of the great commission in the Old Testament. He would not send out missionaries as the New Testament church did, but would build a nation where God's righteousness and justice would flow and the nations do as the Queen of Sheba did with Solomon, when she said "Praise be the God of Israel because of the land that is evidence of who he is." Therefore, the promised land is key to the fulfilling of the Great Commission in the Old Testament. So now after hundreds of years they are poised on the very edge of the land. What a time in the life of this nation! What an excitement fills the people! What an opportunity to be on the edge of the promised land! But then the unexpected happened. The fearful report of the unfaithful spies spreads through the people. "We seem like grasshoppers in our own eyes and we look the same to them." The question they asked was if they should go into the promised land — but the real question was how to possess the land.

This generation for the church is much like that generation for Israel. This is the beginning of the second generation after World War II. It has been 40 years since the treaty was signed. This second generation is in a position of immense opportunity for our local churches in mission. The issue is whether the church will make the same mistake that Israel made by asking the wrong question. The question is not, "will the second generation after World War II be reached with the Gospel?" The question is not "if" but "how?" God's heart still aches for a lost world. We have incredibly good news in Jesus Christ. He has given us courage and power to share this good news. How can we reach this generation? It will take a drastic shift in church strategy.

This generation has inherited a church that has been crippled in its ability to do ministry outside of its four walls. Few argue with that statement, including Baptists in the Bible belt, Mennonite Brethren in the Midwest, Mennonites on the East Coast and charismatics on the West Coast. The church has become a commissary for people with middle class interests. When people are asked, what comes to your mind when you think of the church in ministry, there is a standard response — worship services, Sunday school classes, youth programs, music ministries, children's clubs, Bible studies, nurseries and church committees. Now there is nothing wrong with those ministries. But why do so few people and churches associate ministry with jails, unwed mothers, the physically handicapped, internationals, indigent elderly, or unchurched high school kids?

Ministry Through Para-Church Groups

Since World War II there has been a virtual explosion of para-church ministries on American soil. Men like Dawson Trotman realized that the church did not have the mindset to minister to the military, so he formed the Navigators to reach that group. The Navigators, Campus Crusade, Teen Challenge, Jews for Jesus, Inter-Varsity, Christian Fellowship, Child Evangelism, Youth with a Mission, Teen Mission, World Impact are only a few illustrations of para- ("alongside of") church ministries that have exploded in the past three decades. Para-church organizations have such a vital ministry because they are clearly focused to meet a particular need, and they train these workers to become specialists in a particular area. The tragedy is that the mainline church has abandoned its mission and ministries to para-church groups. In 2,000 years of church history no generation has tried to fulfill the Great Commission through para-structures like the last generation. So much so, that the current mindset among Christian young people essentially says it is the para-ministries that are the fishers of men and the church is the keeper of the aquarium. The para-ministries are on the cutting edge, while churches have adopted fortress mentality, maintaining a certain handful of programs with an incredibly hopeless bureaucratic structure.

If the church is going to seize the enormous opportunities of ministry to a new generation, people will have to be unleashed in service. The church will have to move outside its walls in ministry. This is not an easy shift for any church to make. When I came to Bear Valley Baptist Church in Denver in 1971, I began to preach a ministry mindset and philosophy. We did not have a ministry outside of our walls for five years. But once the people caught the mindset and once the ministries outside the walls began to happen, the church exploded. Today we have 15 major ministries in this city beyond the walls of our church. We are targeting cults, unwed mothers, jails, indigent elderly, street kids, internationals, and artists. Our people have caught on how to use the church as a base of operation to penetrate our world rather than viewing the church as a holy huddle to retreat from society.

Overcoming External Giants

Numbers 13 talks about giants in the land that kept Israel from possessing the land. There are external giants that keep the church from being unleashed in ministry.

At a recent conference in Portland, Oregon, a national leader said, "This generation is a mess." What did he mean? Several months ago a study was done on the most common disciplinary action problems in American schools as perceived by the teachers. They compared this with a similar study done in the early 1940s. In the early 1940s, just after World War II, the problems in our schools were: talking, chewing gum, making noise, running in the halls, getting out of turn in line, wearing improper clothing and not putting waste paper in the basket. The most recent study says our current problems are rape, robbery, assault, burglary, arson, bombings, murder, suicide, absenteeism, vandalism, extortion, drug and alcohol abuse, gang warfare, and pregnancy. Things have changed. Perhaps you saw the recent, heart-wrenching NBC television documentary on child sexual abuse in America. The commentator made this statement. "It's been an average week in the United States, not a bad week, just an average week. This week 5,000 children were abused sexually by pornographers. This week 2,000 kids ran away from home and will become involved in some kind of prostitution. This week in the United States 40 kids were kidnapped, sexually abused and murdered. Not a bad week — just an average week."

These are some of the giants that face the church in our land. Prisons are overflowing. People are broken. There are all kinds of subcultures that the church hasn't even seen. One of the greatest opportunities for world evangelism today has nothing to do with sending missionaries overseas. It involves building a strategy to reach students who are sent to study in our universities from countries all over the world. They are the future leaders of their countries. The one country that is going to double the foreign student population in this country alone, in the next 10 years, is Red China. They are hungry for technological skills. But there are very few churches that have strategy, a plan, a heartbeat and a commitment to look beyond their four walls and to capitalize on the great opportunity.

Overcoming Internal Giants

But the giants that keep the church from being unleashed are not only external. They are primarily internal.

One such internal giant is structural paralysis. Churches don't know how to strategize. One of the differences between the para-movements and the church is that para-groups are strategy oriented. They know who they want to reach and they build strategies to reach them. The local church must switch from being event oriented to becoming strategy orientated or it will be left far behind in this rapidly changing age.

The church has incredible resources in the professional specialists that are part of the body of Christ. Last year at Bear

Valley we started a ministry to the physically handicapped. It was started by a lady who was an occupational therapist. We have the people with the skills and the heart for ministry. Everywhere churches make the fundamental mistake of letting congregations run the church and hiring pastors to do the ministry. We must find pastors whom we trust enough to let them lead the church so that lay people can do the ministry.

The giant of structural paralysis can be overcome by personalizing ministry and strategizing a specific target group. For example, the following is an excerpt of a letter from a person who was reached by a family at Bear Valley. It reads:

Dear Pastor Frank,

Thank you for all the help that people at Bear Valley Baptist Church gave me. I really appreciate the financial help in the home and that the family of Val and Arnie Snyder have given to me. Nicole and I are doing fine. She now weighs 8 pounds 2 ounces and is growing like a weed. There may be a possibility I may have a job this week. Thanks again. I'll write later. Love, so-and-so of Nebraska.

The story behind the letter is heartrending. Like many teens in this country, this girl left home at age 18 over a disagreement with parents. She said, I don't need all this discipline, I can come home whenever I want to and if you don't let me do that, I'll just go to the city. She hitchhiked to the city, met a fellow who invited her to live with him. Everything seemed to work out all right until she told him she was pregnant. Three or four months into the pregnancy, after repeated physical abuse, her boyfriend literally threw her out of the apartment. She was sitting on the front lawn, weeping with her clothes strewn around her, when Christian neighbors picked her up, and invited her into their living room. Their house was full, so they called Bear Valley; We have a target ministry in our church to unwed mothers which includes shepherding homes. People are ready to open their homes to girls in crisis pregnancy until the babies are born. She went to live with Arnie and Val Snyder and for the first time she saw how a Christian husband and wife treat each other. For the first time she saw how Christian parents treat their children. For the first time she was invited to worship with a group of people that preaches Jesus. She opened up her heart to this Jesus and committed her life to Him. The baby was born prematurely, weighing only several pounds. A group of people surrounded her and the baby in prayer. After a month in the hospital the parents and daughter were reunited in Nebraska.

The giant of structural paralysis is overcome when we see the needs of people and move toward them in ministry. For example, in Hutchinson, Kansas there is a state prison that has 92 inmates who have no connection with the outside world. They receive no letters, nor visitors from the outside. The chaplain is looking for Christians to befriend these people through the mail or visitation. These 92 isolated people become a target group for ministry.

The opportunities for ministry in both rural and urban places are endless. A pastor from a small rural town shared with me their use of the target group approach to reach "red-neck cowboys." Somebody came up with the idea of having a trail ride. Since the pastor was a cowboy, they asked him to lead. Friday night they had a trail ride and they brought along a Christian cowboy to give his testimony around the fire. They rode all day Saturday and interacted with these men. Instead of coming back for church Sunday, they held a little worship service around the campfire. Suddenly a group of cowboys who had been unreached started coming to church.

Another giant that keeps the church from being unleashed in ministry is the rural psyche. The problem is not that a rural psyche is good and an urban psyche is bad. It is that different contexts require different strategies. For instance, I grew up with a rural psyche which places tremendous value on the status quo. Howard Heinrichs from Dallas Seminary says status quo is Latin for "the mess we's in." In rural areas stability and sameness have high value. In an urban mindset one must understand change and transition. I am beginning to understand why the Holy Spirit in His wisdom put no structure or methodology into the New Testament church. We know little about how or where they worshiped—except that it was the first day of the week. The Holy Spirit allowed the church to be free to let every generation adopt a structure and a methodology to match the needs of the mission field.

The city church cannot continue to function in a rural mold. One of the sad commentaries is that so many churches look alike. They have the same worship hour, hymns, order of service, Sunday school pattern, men's meeting, leadership training program, and organizational style. God is a God of creativity who wants to produce something beautiful, different and unique. Man, not God, has produced the standardized assembly line church stereotype. Change is always more confusing and complex. At Bear Valley one worship service starts at 8:00 a.m. and the second one begins at 8:30. A lady, who looked in the Yellow Pages, said "this is the shortest service I've ever seen in my life." What she did not understand was that one service begins upstairs in the Fellowship Hall and tends to be more informal, with guitar music, handclapping and no ties or pews. The 8:30 a.m. service is held in the auditorium, and has an order of worship, a choir, and people wear ties and sit in pews. They run concurrently; one from 8:00 to 9:30, the other 8:30 to 9:30, to accommodate different people.

Another giant that must be overcome if the church is to be unleashed in ministry is the corporate mindset. The most frequently used analogy to describe the people of God in New Testament is the church as an organism, or a body. Today the church looks more like a corporate structure. The diagramming of church organizational patterns reflects the bureaucracy of the corporate structures in society.

Recently, I was invited to do a Friday night and Saturday seminar in a city. The person who called me asked me to come a day early to meet with the church board. The board was made up of the 10 committee chairmen who basically ran the church. When the meeting time came there was scripture reading and prayer. Before the minutes from the last meeting could be read one board member said "I'd like to ask, Mr. Chairman, what is this guest doing here?" The chairman indicated the guest had been invited to help the board strategize to have an impact on the city. The man protested, "This is the business of the church, no guest should be invited to this meeting." The chairman graciously responded with, "In any case, he's here, so read the minutes, let's start the meeting." "Just a minute, Mr. Chairman, I don't think it's appropriate that he be here, I think he should be asked to leave and I insist on taking a vote." Meanwhile, I'm sitting there, right in the middle of this debate. There is one thing you have to understand about me, I have an enormously strong ego. My mother told me I was the greatest thing that ever happened. I decided my mother wouldn't lie. So they took a vote. Two people vote that I should leave, four vote I should stay and four abstained. Isn't that great? I don't have much to tell you about the ministry of that church.

What a contrast that story is from some churches I visited in Mexico to urge them to minister outside the fortress, on the campus, to unwed mothers, street kids and bar patrons. During the break two fellows came to talk to me. One still had the lines of alcoholism etched in his face. He said, "Frank, I'm in my mid 50s, I became a Christian three years ago, and stopped drinking when I became a Christian. After I was sober for a year, I felt led of the Lord to go back to the bars to tell my old drinking friends what had happened to me and this brother is coming along with me to keep me accountable. We have just built a ministry in the bars of this city and you're the first person who has ever encouraged us in that. We want to tell you how deeply grateful we are." And as I watched them turn around, the younger man threw his arm around the older man and I asked myself, "What is the difference between these two men and those two board members?" The difference is simple. These two are front line ministers. And those two board members are rear echelon bureaucrats.

Is the church called to develop ministers or rear echelon bureaucrats? Our corporate mindset is killing ministry beyond the four walls of the church. If you say to Navigators or Campus Crusade, "There is a military base, there is an apartment complex, go have a ministry," they know what to do. But if you say the same to a Baptist, Mennonite, Presbyterian or Brethren church most members do not have the faintest idea of how to minister to those groups. They are waiting to be elected at the next annual meetings to some group who is going to oversee the project. Churches do not need all those committees and boards to supervise their work; members need to be involved in ministry. At Bear Valley we have had an attendance of 1,400 people, conducted five services, organized four Sunday schools, managed all kinds of money and mission budgets, and developed 15 major ministries in the city. We have done this with one board, which is elected annually. There are more boards and committees than the main Board of Deacons; but structures must flow out of ministry not vice versa.

There are parallels between what happens in the military and in the church. A man who fought in the Korean War said on the front lines men fought together with one objective—to defeat the enemy. He said, however, when one went 10 miles behind the front lines the whole atmosphere was different. Everybody in the rear echelon was griping and complaining about the weather, the food, the officers, and the conditions. People on front-line ministries function differently than those in the rear echelon. One of the geniuses that God has led us to in our ministry is some strategies and some principles to keep people in front line ministries. Therefore, one of our principles of ministry is that responsibility and authority always go together. We never ask rear echelon people to sit down and decide the responsibility for a particular group and then go out to recruit somebody to do that ministry. If people have the responsibility for ministry, they should have the authority to do it. This principle always produces a dynamic structure, because the people who are structuring ministries are the ones doing them.

Churches must learn to structure, so that chairman or elders or evangelism boards are not doing the ministry. In a seminar I was conducting, a person raised his hand to ask what he should do as chairman of the community outreach committee. My response was, "Think, think about it." Why do so many churches of 100 people elect five people to the community outreach committee? The message this gives to the people is that if God wants to lead this church into ministry, He will tell the outreach committee and the committee in turn tells the people what to do. This cuts off the creativity and spontaneity and the energy of 95 percent of the church.

While I am deeply committed to evangelism, one of the best things most churches could do is destroy their evangelism committees. The message to the whole church is that no one group will carry that monkey on its back for evangelism — everybody listens to the Holy Spirit. Everybody allows their heart to get broken. Everybody stands before God. And if God wants to lead persons into an area of evangelism, He doesn't have to go through the committee to do it. God can speak to you and the church will honor, trust, recognize and build around that ministry.

The problem that repeats itself without fail in church structures is that the most committed people are elected to committees. The result is that those people are not available for front line ministries. They become bureaucrats. The church reaches to others to do the ministry the committee projects, but there is a major motivational problem. The problem is that the people who are doing the ministry had no part in the vision that got it started. Therefore, if the ministry fails, the committee members are at fault because they originated the idea. Authority and responsibility must be lodged with the people who have a heartbeat for a ministry.

Numbers 13:30 says, "Caleb silenced the people before Moses and said, we should go up and take possession of the land, we can certainly do it." The impact on our culture does not lie with the churches with super facilities or with super pastors. It lies with the churches with average pastors and average facilities and average commitment. God loved the ordinary, that is why he created so many of us. And the secret is to turn the average church into a potential center for ministry. Caleb said, "we can certainly do it."

A few years ago a young doctor in our church prayed "God, if you'll send a doctor along to share my suburban practice, I'll donate that half of the practice to the inner city." He had come to the conviction that he could live on half his income. Have you ever met a doctor that couldn't live on half his income? Has there ever been a doctor that was willing to? So he prayed and the word went out to other medical people about this young doctor's dream to build an inner city medical clinic. The volunteer response from doctors, nurses, property owners, psychiatrists, medical equipment distributors was overwhelming. One dentist said, "I have some chairs, drills and needles I will donate." Several Christian nurses volunteered a half day at the clinic. Another dentist donated one day of service a week to the downtown clinic. A Christian psychiatrist said "I am about to retire, I will come down and work at the clinic." A little over a year ago the church opened a full fledged medical clinic in the poorest black section of Denver. It provides dental and medical care, Christian counseling, and Bible studies for the neighborhood kids at night. On Christmas Day, 1984, the Rocky Mountain News ran a front page story of the clinic, located at 34th and Downing. They entitled the article, "The Miracle of 34th Street." It illustrates that there is no limit to what the average church, with average leadership, can do if it becomes unleashed in total commitment under the headship of Jesus Christ.

Questions and Ideas for Discussion

1. Do you agree with the assumption of this chapter, that the call to be a Christian is also a call to ministry? Discuss the biblical evidence and practical implications.

2. What can churches learn from para-church organizations?

What is the relationship between your local church and para-church agencies?

3. How has the giant of structural paralysis hindered ministries in your local church? How can people be unleashed for ministry?

4. How can a church move from "committee-initiated evangelism" to a more "personally-initiated, ministry approach" and still maintain accountability coordination and follow-through in helping people.

5. What "front-line" ministries have been started in your church in the last two years?

6. List some of the unmet needs and unreached people groups in your local community.

6

The Spirit's Empowerment in the Third Way

Henry A. Ginder

Evangelism and church growth are vitally linked to the work of the Holy Spirit. In John 16 Jesus promised his followers the gift of the Holy Spirit. The Spirit's ministry would not only be that of comforting, encouraging, guiding, and empowering believers, but his work in the world was "to convict . . . of guilt in regard to sin and righteousness and judgment" (John 16:8). The Holy Spirit is the greatest evangelist in lifting up Jesus, and in drawing people into the Kingdom. The Holy Spirit continues his work of nurturing growth and preparing believers for effective service. Without the Spirit's anointing, guidance, and empowerment, any evangelistic involvement becomes fruitless human effort.

In thinking about the Spirit's empowerment among churches of the Third Way, it is important to underscore that the dynamic of the gospel message is in reality the power of the Holy Spirit. Evangelism was defined by the Berlin Congress on Evangelism in 1966 as "the proclamation of the whole gospel to the whole world by the whole church." A significant part of the "whole gospel," which evangelical Anabaptists proclaim, is the work of the Holy Spirit in preparing people to receive and share good news.

Two texts focus the role of the Holy Spirit in the evangelistic task of the church of the Third Way. Both Acts 1:1-8 and Colossians 1:28-29 speak about the importance of two dimensions of the Holy Spirit's ministry in evangelism: 1) the command to wait for empowerment, and 2) the command to work with empowerment.

The Command to Wait for Empowerment

Jesus' instructions to the disciples in Acts 1:4-5 were clear, " . . . He gave them this command, do not leave Jerusalem, but wait for the gift my father promised . . . In a few days you will be baptized with the Holy Spirit." They were to take seriously his command—"do not leave Jerusalem." When Jesus commands, his followers need to pay attention, because the spiritual advancement of the church is contingent upon obedience to his directions. In this scripture Jesus gives a promise "You will be baptized with the Holy Spirit." He also makes a prediction "You will be my witnesses." (v. 8)

The trouble with many people in the church is that we want to go before we have come. We want to work before we have waited. We want to preach before we have prayed. Effective evangelism is always prepared evangelism—a heart prepared by the Holy Spirit to listen (e.g., Ethiopian eunuch) and a heart prepared by the Holy Spirit to share (e.g., Philip) (Acts 8:26–40). Today there is too much evangelistic activity and anxiety in churches without the waiting, the prayer, the quietness, the dependence upon the Spirit's empowerment.

The fullness of the Spirit in one's life certainly influences one's zeal to lead others to Jesus Christ. Personally I received the fullness of the Spirit when I was a young man, age sixteen. Immediately I had a strong urge to lead someone to Jesus Christ. My one brother, Amos, was eight years my junior. While working in our father's barn together I asked Amos one day, "Would you like me to help you become a Christian?" He said, "Yes." We sat down together and with my very limited ability, but with the help of the Holy Spirit, I lead Amos to faith in Christ. He was my first convert. He later died as a missionary in Africa.

During the days while I served as Bishop for the Brethren in Christ, a young man called long distance. He requested to see me so that I might help him enter into this rich life in the Holy Spirit. His motivation was clearly stated. He said, "I witness to people regularly in the factory where I work, but no one finds Jesus. If I function in the fullness of the Spirit, I believe someone should be converted. Something must be missing in my life." After a visit together in my office where we shared the Word and prayed for the Spirit's anointing, he returned home. The next week he telephoned again with a different report. He said even though he witnessed the same as before there was a new sense of power and boldness. Already that week he had been instrumental in helping three people find Christ. These simple illustrations point to the fact that we need to observe the command to wait. We need each to experience the fullness of the Holy Spirit.

It is encouraging these days to see how the Holy Spirit is sovereign in bringing many secular people to faith in Jesus Christ. I have seen people receive assurance of salvation without praying with great theological correctness. I have seen God use the very weak among us to successfully bring others to Jesus. For example, I knew a successful pastor who shared how he had invited a wealthy businessman to the Sunday evening service. In their church they had a young man who was not totally capable mentally. The pastor was embarrassed when he heard this deficient young brother talk to his businessman friend and suggest, "You ought to stay and pray, you know it might not hinder but it surely can't help." The young man had mistakenly interchanged the words "help" and "hinder," which made this a very confusing invitation. However, Monday morning the businessman called the pastor for prayer. The pastor inquired of him, "what was it in my sermon that brought you to call for prayer?" The business friend said, "Oh, it was not your sermon, Pastor, it was the sincerity of that young man." Even though his witness was confusing and limited, the Holy Spirit used a weak vessel to bring that business man to salvation. The Holy Spirit is always the key to effective evangelism.

The Command to Work with Empowerment

A second challenge which comes to churches of the Third Way is to the call to work with empowerment. Paul's testimony in Colossians 1:28–29 is powerful. "We proclaim Him, admonishing and teaching everyone with all wisdom, so that we may present everyone perfect in Christ. To this end I labor, struggling with all his energy, which so powerfully works in me." In this passage, Paul illustrates the Holy Spirit's role in evangelism in five important functions of proclamation, discipling, maturing, persevering and empowering.

Paul states clearly "We proclaim Him." In discussions on evangelism today, much is made about the need for presence and performance. Obviously we need to be with people and do good. The Gospels remind us that "Jesus went about doing good." Some of us just go about. The church must model the faith with visible presence and active caring. The Mennonite Central Committee has provided an excellent model of sharing the gospel through presence and performance. Recently Peter Dick, former MCC director stated, "Today there are over 900 trained, dedicated, committed people in MCC, working in 51 countries of the world." God is to be praised for the performance of these dedicated people. However, in the Colossian text Paul emphasized the importance of a theology of proclamation in our witness. There must be a willingness to "proclaim Him." It is true that we proclaim him by our good deeds but we need to interpret and announce who Jesus is. We proclaim him by preaching, by personal witness, by counseling, by music, by drama — by every legitimate means. Our goal is to help people respond personally to the good news of reconciliation.

Proclamation refers not only to formal preaching but to informal contacts and conversation. For example, a ministerial colleague, P. W. McBeth, frequently travels by air to conduct services in different churches. On one occasion he requested an aisle seat but was told that there was none available so he sat in the center. When the stewardess served coffee, there was a bad combination of a slanted table and air turbulence. The end result was that the coffee spilled all over his light gray suit. The stewardess helped in every way possible and then said to Paul, "There is a seat right back of you at the aisle." (This was really what he wanted in the first place.) As he shifted to that seat a young business executive sitting next to him said, "You handled that very nicely." Paul affirmed the stewardess and said that it was really not her fault. The business executive said, "But I would like to have what you have that would enable me to handle a situation like that." Paul explained to the man that he was a Christian, and in what way that affected his attitudes, actions and reactions. He then asked the businessman if he would consider becoming a Christian. Paul was able to lead the business executive to a personal faith in Jesus. They exchanged addresses and Paul discipled him by mail. This only illustrates how the Holy Spirit often provides informal settings for proclamation.

This sharpens the assignment of the church in discipling new converts. Paul says, "they were admonished and taught — every one of them with all wisdom." This takes patience on the part of the Christian doing evangelism. It also calls for perseverance. When people are born again, they receive an "obedient heart." However, even though conversion can be an instant experience, there is no such thing as instant maturity. New converts should be received into the church, in spite of weakness and immaturity. The church is called to foster good body life when people can be nurtured and strengthened in the faith.

The purpose of every church should be to "present everyone perfect in Christ." People need to be brought to maturity and completeness. Spirit-filled persons have a "perfect purpose" to do God's will but they do not always have a "perfect performance." Paul reminds us of this fact with 2 Corinthians 4:7. "But we have this treasure in jars of clay to show that this all surpassing power is from God and not from us." What a lofty purpose! What a challenge for churches to strive to "present everyone perfect in Christ."

"To this end I labor, struggling with all the energy." The great challenge of implementing the learning from conferences such as "Alive '85" is always before us. The application of truth is a constant struggle. It is easy to become discouraged when people's performance is low and evangelism strategies fail. Paul calls us to persevere — to struggle with all the energy that God himself gives. Thus moves one from futility to fruitfulness.

One of our sons and his family served as a missionary in Africa for 12 years. They were originally interested in a pastorate in their North American home church but the task seemed overwhelming. When they returned from Africa, they entered into the home church pastorate, "struggling with all their energy." The Holy Spirit miraculously "broke open" that situation so that the church grew from 70 to 350 in the next several years. In that growth process he indicated that often unconverted church attenders would invite their unsaved friends to church and urge them to become Christians before they themselves had made a commitment to Christ. It is encouraging to see the Holy Spirit do things beyond human effort and expectation.

The phrase "which so powerfully works in me," refers to the energy of God by his Spirit. This is strong terminology. All of us need to confess that we are weak without the Holy Spirit's energy. Myron Augsburger's book, entitled *Practicing the Presence of the Holy Spirit*, is a practical directive for all Christians. It is Biblical, contemporary, practical and really helpful in terms of understanding how the Spirit empowers believers.

Receiving the Spirit's Empowerment

The question naturally arises, "How can one receive the

fullness of the Holy Spirit?" While it is true that every Christian has the Holy Spirit; it is one of God's laws that he cannot give himself to us in fullness until we give ourselves to him in fullness. Every growing Christian, regardless of his theological pilgrimage, has at one time or another craved for a deeper relationship in Christ, and a greater awareness of the Spirit's power. While the Spirit's fullness does not come in easy formulas or neat packages, there are positive steps that every believer can take to open one's life to God's empowerment. First, there needs to be a confession of need for cleansing and filling. Every unholy area in life must be brought to the cross. Second, conscious surrender to Jesus Christ is imperative. Third, thank God in faith for the gift of the Holy Spirit's presence and empowerment. Fourth, claim the Spirit's power for boldness in daily witness.

The evangelistic task of the church cannot be accomplished without the dynamic of the Holy Spirit as the motivating force. There is a barrenness to Christianity that seeks to function without the energy of the Holy Spirit. A personal encounter with Jesus Christ can result in "All His energy so powerfully working in us." The effect will be unmistakably clear in our walk, our witness, our prayers, and our proclamation. The words of Dr. Donald McGavran will become reality, "The Holy Spirit can do more through you in a half day than you can do without Him in a half of a life time." As churches of the Third Way take seriously Jesus' command to wait for empowerment and to work with the Spirit's anointing, "the Word of God will keep on spreading and the number of disciples will continue to increase greatly" (Acts 6:7).

Questions and Ideas for Discussion

1. The command to wait for empowerment is a specific directive. What are some practical ways of "waiting"?

2. Is witnessing natural for all who are filled with the Holy Spirit? (Acts 1:8).

3. Should every Spirit-filled Christian be involved in evangelism?

4. Discuss the experience of the young man who traveled a long distance for help in receiving the Spirit's fullness?

5. How is your congregation working to—"present everyone perfect in Christ"?

6. Discuss ways of practicing the presence of the Holy Spirit.

7. Discuss the four steps to God's empowerment.

8. Is all barrenness in Christianity related to lack of energy in the Holy Spirit?

The Meaning of Conversion in the Third Way

John H. Neufeld

In *Freedom for Ministry*, Richard Neuhaus refers to "the church in all its thus-and-so-ness, its contradictions and compromises, its circus of superficiality, and its moments of splendor."[1] In 15 years of pastoring local congregations I know first hand what Neuhaus is saying, and yet I strongly affirm the local church.

The local church is "where it's at" in terms of accountability, nurture, mutual support, and fellowship. It is in the local church where God's Word is proclaimed from week to week; where Christian education is offered for persons of all ages; where face-to-face sharing and fellowship are experienced; where sins will be confessed and forgiveness received; and where the transition moments of life will be celebrated. It is within the body that is the local church that persons will be invited to become pilgrims of the Christian way. Alfred C. Krass aptly noted that "the congregation of believing Christians is the primary means of spreading the good news."[2]

Since the local church is the setting for telling, doing, and being the community of good news, it is also the setting in which the church needs to reflect on its praxis of evangelism and articulate its understanding of conversion. The need to do ordered thinking about these dimensions of Christian truth and experience is a need arising out of experience.

For example, one day an older person in our congregation shared with me that though she had thought of herself as a Christian for many years, her being a Christian was placed in doubt by the question of a casual acquaintance, "When were you born again?" She could not give time or place and subsequently began to doubt her own Christian experience. In her thinking the question was, "How could I be a Christian if I don't even know when I became one?"

That conversation reminded me of my own experience as a high school student. I too was one of those who could not point to a Pauline-type conversion. The best I could do was refer to a span of about four months in recounting my own conversion. Hearing fellow students give precise accounts of conversion, I doubted whether I was in fact a Christian. I vacillated between doubt and assurance for a long time on the issue of conversion. That which was a personal issue for me 34 years ago is still a problem for many, and needs to be dealt with in churches of the Third Way.

Another question that experience places before the church is the question of children and their decisions for Christ. Young people in membership classes have recalled their childhood experiences and wondered, "Am I a Christian on the basis of that experience?" How does the earlier decision relate to later post-adolescent decisions? Do we agree with Child Evangelism Fellowship on original sin, and accountability, or do we follow the Anabaptist understanding of children?

Another practical reason for addressing the conversion issue is dealt with helpfully by Marlin Jeschke in *Believer's Baptism for Children of the Church*. He makes a distinction between the experience of those who have come to faith as second or third generation Christians, and those who come to accept Christ without having had "pre-decision nurture." Jeschke argues, "the better the job a Christian home and church do in nurturing children, the less likely it is for their children to have the kind of dramatic crisis conversion the New Testament pattern represents."[3] What are our theological and experiential expectations? Are they different for people of different backgrounds? Do we glory in the "trophy catch" of someone who, after having sinned vigorously, has finally accepted the Lord, rather than glorying in the many who come to conscious faith along the less turbulent nurture route?

The purpose of this chapter is to address these questions relating to conversion under three main topics: 1) Biblical Words and Images of Conversion. 2) Paul's Experience as a Model of Conversion, 3) Conversion as a Series of Turning Points.

Biblical Words and Images of Conversion

The Bible has a wealth of material on conversion, both in the Old and New Testaments. The concept of conversion is deeply rooted in a group of words derived from the Hebrew word for "return," and "turn back," "umkehr," (*Shubh*). The "returning" has a specific reference to the covenant (*Bund*) relationship established between God and his people. The covenant is the foundation of Israel as a religious community. It describes Israel's relation to the Lord in a way similar to the relation of a king and his vassals in the late Bronze Age. Exodus 20 is a summary of the Covenant. The main items are: 1) the preamble, "I am the Lord your God," 2) the historical prologue "who brought you out of the land of Egypt," and 3) the stipulations, "You shall have no other gods before me . . ." etc. Later when the people were reminded to give up idol worship and called to repentance, they were specifically called to "return" to the arrangements stipulated in the covenant. This meant that the invitation to conversion or return was limited primarily to the people of the covenant.

Paul Loffler[4] summarizes the Old Testament use of return as follows in four concepts. First, conversion is participation in a historic movement. *Shubh* refers as much to a given event in the past, to a turning point in history which the people must reaffirm again and again, as it refers to the goals of God's action in history. The frequent use of "the way" metaphor is characteristic. Israel has been called to be a people of the way, which is constantly challenged to return to its servant role among the nations moving on behind its Lord.

Secondly, conversion in the Old Testament depends entirely on God's initiative. It is preceded by the givenness of the covenant. God, as the Lord of that covenant, always determines the relationship with his people. Prophets and priests are but his mouthpiece. He himself has to draw Israel back into the reality of covenant. He himself renews the heart and spirit of human beings. Conversion is not a human attempt at appeasement but God's offer of a new beginning after his judgment.

Third, as part of the covenant, Old Testament conversion has primarily a collective connotation. Not that this would completely exclude a personal use of *Shubh*. In the Psalms we find personal confession and repentance. But even there we know that the "I" of the Psalmist is that of a "typical" person, who stands for the whole of the covenant people. On the other hand, the call to return addressed to Israel clearly concerns each of its members personally.

And finally, conversion always involves a vertical response. It does not refer to an affirmation of abstract beliefs but concrete obedience and a renewed relationship in history. What is expected of Israel is to follow a risky political course in the midst of threats from mighty nations, the renunciation of military power, the giving up of idols which promise security and stability. The reality of conversion to God is tested by service to neighbors.

Conversion in the New Testament

The term "return" (*Shubh*) is taken up in the New Testament by two Greek terms, *epistrephein* and *metanoein*. The first one frequently means the physical turning of a person, but is also used in "they turned to the Lord" (Acts 9:35). The second term is often translated "repent" which means "to change one's mind or being". Taken together these words speak of the "turning of the total being to God" away from the powers of darkness, sin and evil.

It is somewhat surprising that these two terms appear infrequently in the New Testament. They are completely absent in the Johannine literature and almost completely absent in Paul's writings. However, it must be pointed out that the meaning of Jesus' coming and his call to His disciples implies a radical turning even though the exact words are not used.

In the synoptic gospels John the Baptist issued a call to repentance (Matt. 3:8) which is inseparably related to ethics. A renewed relationship with God means a new relationship with one's neighbors. Jesus' announcement, "the kingdom is at hand" is the decisively new context for conversion in the New Testament: "The time is fulfilled and the Kingdom of God is at hand: Repent and believe in the Gospel" (Mark 1:15). The "Kingdom" (the rule of Christ) replaces the Covenant of the Old Testament as the framework within which conversion takes place.

In the book of Acts conversion stories differ in details (the Ethiopian eunuch, Lydia, Cornelius, the Philippian jailer, Paul) but in each case conversion is essentially commitment "to the Lord Jesus Christ." Always, conversion is more than a mere change of mind. It is a concrete change to a new way of life, a turning in one's tracks and going in a new direction.

In the Pauline letters there are new terms. Paul uses *pisteuein* (to begin to believe, to become a believer) as the word for conversion. Faith is a response to what God has already done through

Christ. Thus, faith must result in personal commitment and works.

In John's writings faith also means response in concrete obedience. John also uses a new set of terms "birth/rebirth"(John 3:5ff.) "born of God" (1 John 5:4) and "children of God" (John 1:12). These phrases do not intend to minimize the need for personal decision (1 John 5:1). Rather they emphasize the continuous "being in Christ" in contrast to an act of instant decision. (Paul also uses this thought-pattern of "being adopted as sons" — Gal. 4:5, Eph. 1:5, Rom. 8:15.)

Paul Loffler correctly concludes by saying, "it is clear the New Testament insists on conversion as a response to God's action in history."[5] He summarizes the Old and New Testament understanding of conversion in five statements. First, conversion is a personal re-orientation to God. God's action in history demands concrete response by historic persons.

Second, while conversion and sanctification cannot be separated, they must be distinguished by definition. "Turn" and "repent" always relate to the beginning, not to the whole process of becoming a Christian. Whereas sanctification refers to an ongoing movement, conversion literally means a particular turning. The Christian life of service and witness is in need of both — conversion and sanctification. One without the other is void.

Third, in the Old Testament, conversion is in the first instance commitment to, and participation in, a movement forward. But in the second (not secondary) way it means also liberation from the past and from the forces and powers of evil. In the Old Testament the prophetic call to conversion always includes an emphatic "no" to idolatry. In the New Testament conversion sets free to a new life in Christ. It is acceptance of forgiveness, based on obedience of faith. Neither the scope nor the significance of conversion can be confined to the narrow personal sphere.

Fourth, the only New Testament basis for conversion is Jesus Christ. Through his coming, re-orientation to God attains a new meaning and historicity. It simply means now to follow him, to enter into his discipleship with the same whole and uncompromising obedience with which he has lived in history.

Fifth, the beginning of the Kingdom through Christ's entry into human history is the main context of conversion in the New Testament. In one of his books Leslie Newbigin has suggested that conversion in the New Testament is a turning around in order to participate by faith in a new reality which is the true future of the whole creation. It is not in the first place either saving one's soul or joining a new society. It means turning around so that one's face is towards Christ. It means being caught up into the activity of God which is directed to that end.

This new reality, the Kingdom of God, breaks into our present from the future. It leaves us with the choice of taking our cues from the past or from the future. When Moses and Aaron instructed the Israelites about the passover they issued an invitation to believe before the evidence was in. The people were asked to turn and live from that moment trusting that Yahweh who had entered their present from the future was trustworthy. They were called to convert from Pharaoh to Yahweh.

In the New Testament Jesus announced the inbreaking of his Kingdom and invited people to believe in Him and the Kingdom He proclaimed. He challenged people to turn, to give up their old loyalties, and to commit themselves to follow as pilgrims on His way.

In both cases, the initial turning was crucial. The decision to trust shaped their existence from that time on. But this initial turning had to be confirmed by many subsequent turnings. "The repentance by which we enter the Way, becomes a pattern of life by which we remain on the Way."[6]

Paul's Experience as a Model of Conversion

Is Paul's conversion pattern the model for persons turning to Christ today? At best, it is one model. It would be interesting to have had Paul and Timothy appear together on a panel: "When did you become a Christian, Paul?" "I remember it as yesterday . . . (Damascus road)." And Timothy? "Well, my grandmother was a Christian, and my mother, and I am one too."

On the basis of Scripture and experience, we would all affirm with John that "the Spirit blows where he wills." There is such a variety of operations. The Lord is not at all limited by one series of steps or another. One experience will not allow us to standardize conversion.

The great variation of experience is illustrated in the Gospels by the four incidents of blind people receiving their sight. In the Bible, blindness is a symbol of being unconverted. It would have been interesting to hear these four men at a news conference re-count their stories of how they received their sight. The first one (Matt. 9:27 ff.) might have said, "I met Him one day and told him I believed he could restore my sight. All He did was touch my eyes and say 'According to your faith be it done to you.'"

The second person's (Mark 8:22ff.) account was different. "My friends took me to this man Jesus and asked him to touch me. He took me by the hand, led me out of the village, spit on my eyes and asked me, 'Do you see anything?' My reply was 'I see men, but they look like walking trees.' So he laid his hands on me again and I saw things clearly."

The third blind man (Mark 10:46ff.), who had been a beggar, gave this report, "I was begging on the roadside and heard people say that Jesus of Nazareth was coming by, so I began to shout 'Jesus, son of David, have mercy on me.' When he came up to the place where I was sitting, I begged, 'Master, let me receive my sight.' All he said was, 'Go your way, your faith has made you whole.' Immediately I received my sight."

Finally, the fourth one spoke: (John 9:1 ff.) "I was blind since birth. When Jesus came by he spat on the ground, made some clay with the spittle and plastered it on my eyes, saying, 'Go wash in the Pool of Siloam.' So I went, washed out my eyes and saw!"

Each one of these four men was converted, from blindness to sight, from darkness to light, from groping to seeing. The details of each were somewhat different but each unique experience was valid. Together they rejoiced that they had received sight and hope. Let us never make one type of experience normal and normative! Let us never impose our experience on others!

A Distinction Between Adult and Child Conversion

In his recent book on "Believer's Baptism,"[7] Marlin Jeschke has argued convincingly that we must distinguish between the usual New Testament pattern of "crossing over" as an adult from the realm of unfaith to an acceptance of Christ and the Christian way, and the movement of a person nurtured in a Christian environment from innocence to owned faith. Paul as well as many others (the Ethiopian eunuch, the Philippian jailer, Lydia, Cornelius) repre-sent the usual New Testament pattern.

Jeschke argues that we must revise our expectations and adapt the New Testament pattern in reference to children who have had the privilege of being raised in a Christian environment. As the young person moves from the period of innocence to the period of discretion and accountability, he/she is faced with a clear alternative: to consciously appropriate and own the faith in which he/she was nurtured, rather than to go the alternate route of disobedience and unfaith.

This decision of a young person to own the faith, to consciously decide to be a follower of Christ and a member of the church, will not necessarily show the contrast of a converted adult. "In the case of children growing up in Christian homes, the beginning of Christian faith is gradual. It is not necessarily an immediate, datable, all-or-nothing proposition, but can be a process over a period of time."[8]

The subtle danger of this view is the assumption that young people growing up in the church do not have to decide whether or not they will be Christian. "To make no decision is to make a decision, the decision not to identify with the Christian way."[9] Young people who have grown up in Christian homes and churches must be confronted with the necessity of a deliberate, conscious choice and commitment.

If we want to use the term "conversion" in a loosely defined way, then we simply affirm the different ways of coming to faith, as in *Christian Conversion in Context,* Hans Kasdorf affirms three different ways of coming to faith as: 1) a conscious, voluntary, gradual rather uneventful move; 2) a sudden crisis experience where a person makes a sudden change in life and relationships; and 3) a long process, occurring in peaks or a series of crisis, some more important than others.[10] Kasdorf continues to speak of "the point of conversion, defined as, the encounter where divine justification and human faith meet. The point at which one decides to follow Christ."[11]

Conversion as a Series of Turning Points

In his insightful book, *Word in Deed*, Gabriel Fackre suggests that conversion or turning is in fact composed of a series of turning points. "Total turning includes a sequence of smaller turns. . . . Authentic Christian reorientation is a full turn that includes four turning points: repent, believe, be baptized, and serve.[12]

Fackre summarizes the meanings of these four turning points. First, repent suggests turning from, away from evil or darkness, i.e., anything which has power over us, because Christ has overcome the powers of darkness, selfishness, and sin. Second, to believe is to have faith that the source of our wrongs has been dealt with, a way back is possible, not by our own merit, but by God's grace. Believing is turning to the light that overcomes the darkness.

The third turning point for Fackre is baptism, one phase of conversion, which marks the process as more than a change of heart and head. It is a change of location providing new relationships and new community. In baptism it is affirmed that the journey is not a solo trip but participation in a company of pilgrims.

Service is another turning point in the conversion process. Conversion begins in repentance and is climaxed in service: sharing the gospel, clothing the naked, feeding the hungry, visiting prisoners, doing justice, making peace.

Fackre concludes by quoting Leslie Newbigin: "Conversion then, means being turned around in order to recognize and participate in the dawning reality of God's reign. But this inward turning immediately and intrinsically involves both a pattern of conduct and a visible companionship. It involves membership in a community and a decision to act in certain ways."[13]

Churches of the Third Way reaffirm the priority of conversion as the doorway into the Kingdom of Christ. We acknowledge the variety of conversion experiences among Christians. No one type of conversion can serve as a necessary paradigm for everyone else. While we affirm the value of childhood decisions, we recognize the necessity of consciously making commitments with a deeper understanding in later adolescence or early adulthood. We believe that conversion is the beginning of the lifelong process of continuously renewing the basic direction of our lives and that we consciously and with joy want to walk in the company of Christ and his people. Churches of the Third Way continue to invite those who have no nurturing background, as well as those who do, to consciously make the four turns of repentance, belief, baptism and service and thus be converted. There is a constant need to reexamine our own assumptions about conversion in the light of Scripture and to strengthen Jesus' teaching that "unless you are converted and become like children, you cannot enter the kingdom of heaven.

Questions and Ideas for Discussion

1. Having read this chapter, reflect on your own experience of coming to faith or being converted. Share your reflections with others.

2. Do you agree with the distinction made between the experience of conversion of those having had Christian nurture, and the expreience of those who accept Christ without previous nurture?

3. Does the review of biblical words and images confirm or challenge your own understandings? Elaborate.

4. What is your own definition of conversion?

5. What are the expectations in your congregation regarding conversion? How are these expressed in congregational life?

6. Do you agree with the conclusions at the end of the chapter? Elaborate.

8

Discipling New Converts in the Third Way

Palmer Becker

The Lord of the harvest has commissioned every believer and church to the task of worldwide evangelism. It is no small task, and calls for our total commitment. Garth Hunt, a long-term missionary and the current director of Living Bibles International, has said, "The Great Commission is not just part of the commission. It is the whole commission! It is what we are called to be and to do. As Christians we are born to a task. We don't have to wait for a challenge. We don't have to wait for a call or a vision. We've already been given that challenge. It's the task of worldwide evangelism."[1]

Churches of the Third Way have placed a high priority on worldwide evangelism. In that evangelism we believe that God is calling us to do more than call for decisions or make converts. Henri Nouwen puts his finger on a truth that we affirm when he says, "God has put the hurting people of the world into the arms of the church."[2]

The task of the church is to bring Christ's healing to hurting people. Our task is to bring these hurting people to Christ with the prayer that they will become whole, mature and ministering disciples. This chapter on "Discipling New Converts in Churches of the Third Way" focuses on two important dimensions: 1) Selecting a few for discipling, and 2) helping these disciples to make a three-fold commitment.

Selecting a Few for Discipling

Jesus is the Master-Discipler. Church leaders had best take their discipling clues from him. In the *Master Plan of Evangelism*, Robert Coleman has aptly noted, "There was nothing haphazard about this man. There was no wasted energy, no idle words. He was on God's business."[3] Jesus was not primarily a prophet or a teacher. He was that but he was more. Jesus was at heart an evangelist and a disciple-maker. His aim was to gather a people into the Kingdom of God. These people, who had been reconciled and empowered by God's love, were to become disciplers. The Kingdom was to be expanded through committed disciplers.

While Jesus did not neglect a ministry to the masses, he repeatedly narrowed his focus to concentrate on a smaller group of disciples. The masses cannot be discipled — they can be taught but not trained. Jesus knew that so he concentrated his energies on a few primary disciples.

The number of people who came into Jesus' life grew rapidly in the first days of his ministry. First, John the Baptist referred two of his new converts to Jesus for follow-up. Their names were John and Andrew. Then Andrew invited his brother, Peter. That made three. The next day they bumped into Philip. Then they recruited Nathanael, who was sitting under a fig tree not particularly gainfully employed. Within a few days Jesus had five people sharing together.

His following continued to grow. Soon 70 disciples gathered around him. They followed him most of the time.[4]At times he was surrounded by crowds that numbered in the thousands. Jesus experienced what could be called "evangelism by attraction." People were attracted because their hurts and needs were being met by someone who cared.

But in spite of the crowds Jesus continually demonstrated the principle of selectivity. Luke 6 records how Jesus called the 70 disciples and chose from among them 12 whom he named as apostles. Even within the group of 12 Jesus narrowed his focus. He chose Peter, James and John to be with him in a very special way. Only these three were allowed into the sick room of Jairus' daughter. Only Peter, James and John were invited to join him on the Mount of Transfiguration. And only these three were with him in his crisis in the Garden of Gethsemane.

Church leaders would do well to study the strategy of Jesus carefully. While the entire congregation and community is important, giving focal attention to a few potential leaders, a membership class of 12 or a group of Bible study leaders is even more strategic. To choose smaller groups for discipling can have far-reaching results. For example, Peter became one of the greatest preachers of all times. Three thousand people responded to one of his messages. James became such a vibrant witness that he was singled out for execution by King Herod. And John, the beloved, has influenced billions through his five books of the Bible.[5]

Because Jesus selected a manageable number, he could conclude his ministry on a note of victory. In his prayer in John 17 he reports to his Father, "I have revealed you *to those whom you gave me* out of the world . . . and they have obeyed your word . . . and have believed that you sent me." Jesus could say "Mission accomplished! These potential disciples that you gave to me are now faithful followers."

Potential disciples need to be chosen carefully. Jesus spent a whole night in prayer before he chose those on whom God wanted him to concentrate. Perhaps each of us has about 70 family members, neighbors, working associates or primary acquaintances. As followers in the Third Way we would do well to choose two or three people that we might disciple for Christ. We are called to be their friends, pray for them by name and pour our life into them! It is choosing and training a few that the masses can be reached. That is how Jesus did it and we are to follow in his steps.

What do we do after we have identified those that we feel are potential disciples?

Helping Disciples Make Three Commitments

The objective of discipling is to draw people into commitment that can be illustrated by three stairsteps. Discipleship involves a commitment to Christ, to Christ's body, and to Christ's work in that order. These three commitments are essential for bringing spiritual and physical wholeness and emotional healing to people.

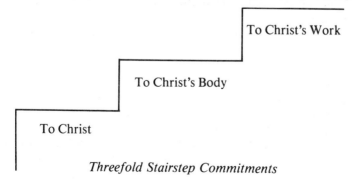

Threefold Stairstep Commitments

A Commitment to Christ

The first commitment a disciple is called to is a personal relationship to Jesus Christ. One cannot be a part of the kingdom without committing oneself to the King. Commitment to the King may happen over a process of time, but it must be specific.

Jesus began by inviting potential disciples with the words, "follow me." The invitation was always personal. It called for willingness, loyalty and faithfulness to the one who leads a movement. Jesus Christ is both the "who" and "what" of the Christian. He is the way to know God and his will. Helping a disciple make a commitment to Christ involves preparation. John Wesley White has said that 45 percent of the discipling process is in the preparation. Ten percent is in the proclamation. And the remaining 45 percent is in the preservation. Someone has said, "The day after a victory is as important as the day before. The day before, we prepare ourselves; the day after, we retain the gain."

During the preparation one needs to earn the right to share a basic understanding of Christ. This establishes contact and confidence. The person feels care and concern. The person gets to know a Christian as a person who is seeking their best welfare.

Christians need to be ready to share the Good News at the appropriate time. We need to be clear about the content of that Good News. Just as a music scale is helpful to a musician who wants to share melodic expression, an outline of the basics can be beneficial in sharing the good news. While an outline of the gospel should always be a servant rather than a master, it can help to both clarify the message and to give the person sharing a greater sense of confidence. An outline could include the following points: 1) God's will. Doing God's will is the most important thing in life. It leads to fellowship, purposeful living, a clear conscience, and a future hope. It is never better not to do God's will. The good news is that God in his grace gives us both the desire and the power to do his will (Matthew 6:10; 7:21). 2) Human will. Doing one's own will is a natural inclination. But it leads to separation and loneliness, to temporal values, purposelessness in life, and to the breaking of relationships with God and fellow man. The bad news of doing our own will is a guilty conscience, loss of hope, and the death of an abundant spirit and life (1 John 2:15–17; Romans 6:23). 3) Christ came to teach and demonstrate God's will. As God's unique and divine prophet, priest and King, He died to pay the penalty for our sins. He rose that we might have his resurrected spirit within us which empowers us to do his father's will (John 10:7-10; 14:12). 4) Human response. The gospel calls people to acknowledge their independence and selfishness, to repent and to turn again to doing God's will. The Good News is that forgiveness and life are possible when there is an honest confession and faith commitment. God promises new life to people who acknowledge their past disobedience, claim Christ's forgiveness and commit themselves to do his will (1 John 1:8-9).[7]

Samuel Shoemaker has described a Christian as one "who surrenders as much of himself as he can to as much of Christ as he understands."[8] This means that to become a disciple a person must choose Christ over other options. Only when a person chooses from among options can he or she cherish the choice and feel good about it. Membership classes can be one context where serious students are faced with the choice between a commitment to Christ as Lord and Master or to humanistic philosophies. Commitment means that individuals clearly confess their sinfulness and make a conscious choice between Jesus and the various false saviors the modern world parades (i.e. money, alcohol, sex, military power and violence). Finally a commitment to Jesus Christ calls people to sort out whom one is going to serve. A person who makes a commitment to Christ clearly affirms, "Jesus is my Saviour, Teacher and Lord."

Discipling Involves Dialoguing with God

A commitment to Jesus Christ becomes personal through daily dialogue with God. A discipler helps his disciple to begin that dialogue. The first half of the dialogue is listening. Disciples need to learn to listen to God. Bible study is the primary way of listening to God.

Linda came to the Peace Church about a year ago very depressed. She was ready to call it quits. She had nothing to live for and hoped to die at an early age. She made a commitment to Jesus Christ and experienced a new sense of fellowship, purpose and eternal destiny. But then her commitment started to fade. It was only when Linda was helped in the discipline of listening to God through the scriptures that her commitment was renewed. She is presently exploring the scriptures in a three year period using the Inter-Varsity book, *Search the Scriptures.*[9] Just recently she said, "I'm enjoying the scriptures so much. God is speaking to me every day!" She is learning to listen to God and enjoys what she is hearing.

The second half of a dialogue is speaking. Prayer is speaking to God. A Chinese proverb says, "Little prayer, little power; no prayer, no power." Jesus knew this truth and his disciples came to know it as well. In desperation they said to Jesus, "Lord, teach us to pray." Jesus did teach them both by his own example (Mark 1:35), and through his words in the Lord's prayer (Luke 7) and his high priestly prayer (John 17). Many churches have found the brochure, "Seven Minutes with God," to be helpful in discipling new converts in their personal dialogue with God.[10]

Some people have a meaningful dialogue with God in tongues. Others pray in English or their mother tongue. Still others communicate with God through music or special meditation. God understands every language but the point is that there must be vital communication with him.

Commitment to Christ with an emphasis on personal relationship and dialogue with God is only the first step. If the disciple does not move on to new levels of commitment, there will usually be a falling away. Churches of the Third Way call people to a second commitment.

Commitment to Christ's Body — The Church

The King has a Kingdom. New converts need to be invited to commit themselves to his lordship and the Kingdom rule. His is a Kingdom of right relationships. This Kingdom is not only future, but it begins on earth as people follow Jesus Christ and identify with his people, the church.

After Jesus invited his first followers to commit their lives to him, he stayed with them. He went on work trips and retreats with them. Together they went to Tyre and Sidon in the northwest; to Cesarea in the northeast; to Jerusalem and Jericho in the South: to the mountain of transfiguration and to Pyrea east of the Jordan. He poured his life into his new community.

It was in the warmth of personal relationships that those first followers of Jesus were nurtured and discipled. They were made strong in the group. Jesus' approach was very person-oriented. He knew his disciples well and they knew him "like a book." Jesus did not tell his disciples to "go spend more time in the closet praying," "go take a doctrines class," or "to go read a book." He invited them to be with him (Mark 3:14). Most new converts need fellowship more than they need knowledge. They need knowledge in the context of warm relationships.

We did a recent study at the Peace Church of people who had found Christ but had not found a "home" in the church. We observed that in every case these new converts had less than three friends in the fellowship. Most of them were totally devoid of primary friends in the church. They had bonded themselves to Christ but the bonding with Christ's body had not taken effect. God's challenge to the church is to provide opportunity for new converts to become part of a cell group for prayer support, encouragement and nurture. Only as committed peer relationships in the Kingdom are formed can we expect converts to continue to grow.

At the Peace Church we are seeking to form covenant groups which call for the following commitments from people: 1) A promise to meet regularly to encourage one another in Christ; 2) A promise to pray regularly for one another; 3) A promise not to criticize one another outside of the group; and 4) A promise to share resources with one another according to need.[11] In a covenant group a new disciple goes beyond the personal guidance from individual study of God's word to the practical counsel from other believers as they study together and apply it. New disciples should not only learn to share their burdens privately with God in prayer, but should also have the opportunity to pray and be prayed for by name in the group.

Research of 500 congregations has indicated that a church grows both in quality and quantity in direct proportion to the number of face-to-face groups in the church.[12] In our particular church we personally invite every attender to be a part of a small group in the fall of each year. The church seeks to be a congregation of groups rather than a congregation of individuals meeting for a Sunday morning service. If the church is to be a place where people can pray together, help each other make decisions, and serve together in mission, then groups of 8-12 people are the best context in which this can happen. The congregation then becomes a cluster of smaller fellowships gathering together for corporate worship and celebration, but meeting separately for more personal sharing, encouragement, prayer and involvement.

Group life is the best glue to hold new converts together. Without this second commitment—a commitment to each other in Christ's body, new disciples will not have the resources or strength for the next step.

Commitment to Christ's Work

After inviting them to personally follow him and after helping followers become a committed group, Jesus put them to work. His first promise was, "I will make you fishers of men." He did not fail in that promise. He sent the twelve and then the seventy into the villages to minister, to heal and to find disciples. They preached the gospel and healed wherever they went. They served as ushers and table waiters at the feeding of the 5,000. At the end Jesus sent them out to the whole known world with the great commission to make disciples. They were well-trained. They were able to reproduce themselves. The disciples had become disciple-makers!

Our task, like Jesus, is to make disciple-makers who have a reconciling ministry. To do this, new converts must know the gospel so that they can invite others to commit their lives to Jesus Christ. They must have a firm rootage in a faith community so that they can draw others into the body of Christ. In the context of that body, new converts need to be helped to formulate a strategy for involvement in Christ's work.

Lyle Schaller, a well-known church consultant, has observed that many established members of a congregation have joined for heritage reasons. They belong to the church because their parents belonged and because their ancestors gave their lives to build the church. By contrast new members tend to join a congregation because they are attracted by its mission and goals. A congregation can be significantly helped and unified by articulating its goals.[13]

Jesus challenged his disciples to walk among people, to see their needs and to minister to their hurts. New converts need to be trained and unleashed in ministry among needy people. Committed converts will do more than study the Bible and be nurtured in the context of a warm small group and church fellowship. True followers of Jesus are marked by a commitment that expresses itself in loving service, compassionate concern and prayerful involvement in the world.

It is important to emphasize caution in moving converts too quickly from step one, commitment to Christ, to step three, commitment to service. A healthy emphasis is needed on step two, commitment to the church. If new believers neglect a strong commitment to Christ's body and seek to do his work without a strong support base, the end result can be disillusionment and lack of spiritual power.

Bill Pannel, a professor at Fuller Theological Seminary, uses three words to describe a disciple's commitment to Christ's work. Disciples are *ethical*. They call people to right living in the face of such great world problems as hunger, racism, war and injustice. Second, disciples are *ecumenical*. Reconciled people work together for wholeness in the face of divisions both in the church and in the world. And thirdly, disciples are *enthusiastic*. They bring new life to discouraged people in the face of tiredness, confusion and fear.[14] It is the discipler's challenge to help new Christ-centered disciples to be ethical, ecumenical and enthusiastic in their daily life and work.

Jesus is the model discipler and the master teacher. By the world's standard he was not totally successful. There were only 11 in his graduating class. Judas failed to make the grade but the other eleven were solid. They went everywhere preaching the gospel and discipling converts.

Jesus reached the masses by carefully training a handful. That is still the most far reaching strategy that church leaders can employ in fulfilling the Great Commission, the orders are clear, "Go . . . and make disciples." The question is, "will leaders follow the strategy of Jesus by selecting a handful of potential disciples and helping them to mature in their commitment to Christ, to Christ's body, and to Christ's work?"

Questions and Ideas for Discussion

1. In your own words, what is the task of the church?

2. How do you respond to the statement, "Jesus was at heart an evangelist and disciple-maker"?

3. What is meant by "evangelism by attraction"? Where have you seen it happen?

4. Do you feel your pastor should be given the encouragement and freedom to concentrate on training a few potential leaders?

5. How do you feel about Samuel Shoemaker's statement, "A Christian is one who surrenders as much of himself as he can to as much of Christ as he understands"?

6. How do you respond to the three commitments outlined in the chapter and to the suggested sequence of those commitments.

7. In a few words jot down a strategy that you would like to follow for discipling new converts and share it with the group.

Friendship Evangelism in the Third Way

Arthur G. McPhee

Evangelism's image is tarnished. For many it has become associated with high pressure salesmanship, or manipulative "love-bombing" when persons are most vulnerable. Most feel uncomfortable with faith-sharing that seems artificial or canned. Evangelism often seems more rooted in guilt and duty than love and spontaneity. If evangelism is sharing good news, then it must be good news both to the people who share it and the people who hear it.

Churches of the Third Way have a high view of Jesus Christ. They view Jesus as Lord and Savior, but they don't stop there. They also look to him as a model of values, lifestyle and evangelism methodology. They recognize that Jesus came into the world not only to share the Good News but to demonstrate how to share it.

One of the greatest compliments the Pharisees paid Jesus, though they meant it as criticism, is found in the words, "The Son of Man is . . . a friend of tax-gatherers and sinners." Jesus was a master at caring for people, bridging communication barriers and meeting people at their point of need — especially their spiritual need, for in the course of natural relationships, he freely shared the Good News with everyone. His approach was never manipulative or overbearing, but his witness was clear and his call to a commitment was decisive. In other words, Jesus saw evangelism as vital — but his evangelism was not a package or a program, it was spontaneous witness in the context of relationships.

Friendship Evangelism: Some Basic Assumptions

There are some basic assumptions, which places the approach of friendship evangelism, not in competition with the various strategies that are employed today, but in the context of general evangelism methodology.

I used to think of friendship evangelism[1] as one strategy

among many employed by local churches. I now believe I was wrong. Whenever friendship is thought of as a method, it ceases to be friendship and is reduced to manipulation. It becomes artificial and even sinful. Take, for example, Christian university students who, during the first days of the academic year, corner lonely, vulnerable freshman in some such setting as the campus dining hall. They sit down with new students, put their arms on their shoulders, and tell them what great persons they are. But since the goal is not really friendship but religious indoctrination, the Christian students are actually exploiting the newcomers' weakness in order to spring the gospel on them. Here's why: They have put the Great Commission (Go, make disciples) ahead of the Great Commandment (First of all, love God and your neighbor). Rather than seeing evangelism as an expression of love and friendship, they see it as an end in itself. Their strategy becomes a clever means to an unsought, perhaps even forced, hearing, rather than an opportunity to create a caring relationship where faith-sharing happens naturally.

I realize the difference is subtle, but I believe it is vital we recognize it if we are to evangelize with the integrity Jesus showed. To do so will not make us less effective in the Spirit's hands, and it will not necessarily mean abandoning present programs. We will continue to use a variety of methods to create opportunities for witness, but we shall never do so under false pretenses nor without regard for the wishes of the persons to whom we witness. This does not limit enthusiasm, earnestness, emotion or persuasive reasoning — only manipulation. That is why friendship cannot be a means (method) but only an end (attitude) that liberates our methods from cultishness, intrusiveness and exploitation.

My second assumption is that friendship evangelism, unlike formal evangelistic strategies, is something every Christian practices. It is not just another option.

The Bible describes Christians with a multitude of metaphors. Followers of Jesus are described as: fishers, salt, light, stars, good seed, ambassadors and witnesses. It is interesting to note that the metaphors are in the Greek indicative mood rather than the imperative. In other words, the Bible doesn't say, "Be salt . . . be light . . . be letters." It says, if you are a Christian, you *are* all these things. If so, what are the implications of such descriptions? First, they suggest that evangelism is not simply a program but a way of life. Second, every Christian is an evangelist, a spontaneous, constant witness to the Good News of the Kingdom.

These metaphors do not assume an evangelism of presence without proclamation and persuasion, however. In the New Testament there are more than 30 Greek verbs that describe various aspects of articulating the faith. If verbalizing the Good News were unimportant and one could manifest it adequately by just living it, those verbs would be fewer and less predominant. And in that case Jesus, who lived a perfect life, would not have needed to proclaim the Gospel for the Kingdom life to which we call persons. The point is that the metaphors assume that being salt and light involves proclamation and demonstration. Both are the natural and normal overflow of our relationship with Christ (John 7:37–39).

Notice further that the salt and light metaphors follow the beatitudes in Matthew's Gospel. The beatitudes describe the characteristics of Christians—they recognize their moral and spiritual bankruptcy; they agonize over their own personal sin and the sins of the world; they are not self-seeking; they hunger for holiness in their lives; they suffer for Christ's sake and are reconcilers. After Jesus lists all these beatitudes, He says "You . . ." In Greek the "you" comes at the beginning the sentence and is, therefore, emphatic. So, it is as if he were saying, "You and you alone are the salt of the earth." "You and you alone are the light of the world." That light is the inevitable overflow of the characteristics of Christians outlined in the beatitudes. So, you cannot be a Christian and not be a witness, it is only an issue of the kind of witness—negative, positive or mediocre.

My third assumption can also be seen in the biblical metaphors that describe Christians. The metaphors make it clear that our impact and effectiveness is in the context of the world. One cannot be light except in the darkness. This implies that Christians are involved in the midst of struggling humanity. Churches of the Third Way have at times confused separation with isolation. We have tried to reach people on our turf rather than going to meet them where they live and work. The implication is that churches must shift from a primary strategy of invitation to a strategy of penetration. It is the difference between New Testament and Old Testament evangelism. In the Old Testament Israel was a light to the nations. Jerusalem was the center; Israel was the showpiece of the one true God—Yahweh. In the New Testament the people of God were sent out to proclaim good news. In fact, persecution came to scatter the early church so that the gospel went to Samaria and Antioch. These people went everywhere gossiping about their faith (Acts 8:4).

In Jesus' high priestly prayer he asked not that his followers be taken "out of this world, but that they would be kept from the evil one" (John 17:15). He goes on in that prayer to make it clear that just as he had been sent into the world by the father, "I also have sent them into the world" (John 17:17). The challenge of friendship evangelism is to maintain one's commitment to Christ's call, value system and basic principles and at the same time to be deeply involved with people whose lives and value systems are totally contrary to Christ's call.

Friendship Evangelism — Lesson From the Gospels

The Gospel writers give us a picture of how Jesus related to people. There are important principles that are illustrated from Jesus' life, and particularly his use of fishing imagery. There are at least five valuable friendship evangelism principles that can be gleaned from Jesus' life. These principles are transferable and applicable to his followers in every age.

Often we think of Jesus as a mass evangelist, but his primary evangelistic methodology was personal. The Gospels record 153 personal encounters of Jesus with individuals who responded to his message. (It is not clear how many of these persons simply came out of the crowd and responded in that preaching context.) What is even more significant is that Jesus spent most of his time with a group of twelve men and a few women who followed him. Within that circle of twelve there was an inner circle of three, Peter, James and John.

The point is that Jesus loved and cared for people wherever he went. While he ministered to the masses, he did so with a personal touch. When he worked with the smaller group of disciples he shared his life in a personal way. In an age that is increasingly technological and impersonal the most powerful communication skill Christians have to offer is a personal interest, touch, words of encouragement, commitment to individual people.

With an amazingly full schedule, with the burden of the world on his shoulders, Jesus still took time for people. Whether it was a woman at the well in Samaria, a tax collector under a fig tree in

Jericho, a ruler's son who needed help, or the training of the twelve, Jesus was available to people.

This has practical implications in terms of the way we do evangelism. It means, for example, that our lifestyle is going to be one that has enough flexibility to love people. It has been said that "people don't care how much we know until they know how much we care." It means that as we move among larger groups of people, we focus on individuals. It means that among the many casual acquaintances we need to be especially sensitive to the few persons that God gives us a burden for. It means the investment of time and energy in a relationship with them.

This is one of the reasons why some people have so few friends. In our society one out of every four people say they have no friends at all. Some time ago I was fascinated by one of Charles Schultz's cartoons. Lucy asks, "Charlie Brown, what do you think you'll be when you grow up?" And Charlie Brown responds, "Lonely." The tragedy of the modern age is that everyone is so busy, we don't take time to cultivate significant relationships.

A third dimension regarding Jesus' approach to people was his call to commitment. He was sensitively straightforward in his appeal. He respected people's integrity whether they answered his call positively or negatively. When the rich young ruler wanted to follow Jesus, he was confronted directly with the challenge to "Sell what you have, give to the poor." Jesus did not beg people to follow him. In fact, when people indicated their interest in following him, he probed further to make sure they understood the nature of their commitment. In other words, his evangelism did not simply lead to decisions, it led to discipleship and obedience.

Jesus made his call to commitment specific. In each instance his call fit the context of the people he encountered. When he met Nicodemus he said, "You must be born again" (John 3); to the woman caught in adultery he said, "Go your way and sin no more" (John 8); to the centurion, whose son was healed his words were "Go your way, your faith has made you whole."

Jesus gave his disciples assignments. He did not wait until they were in the church 10 years before they were given any kind of responsibility. He sent them out two by two to announce the fact that he was coming.

Salvation, in the Scriptures, is described as a process involving the past (Titus 3:5), the present (1 Corinthians 1:18), and the future

(1 Peter 1:5). It is a process that begins when we make the decision to follow Christ, but is not complete until we are called home. We are being fitted for heaven throughout our lives.

Jesus gave his disciples assignments to help them grow and mature. He supervised them in these assignments. They came back, reported their experiences, Jesus evaluated their reports and gave further directives.

A final principle from Jesus' life is that he prayed for his disciples and encouraged them. He interceded for their spiritual alertness; for their protection from the evil one, for their relationships with one another, and for their witness in the world (John 17).

Friendship evangelism is more than befriending people. It is prayerfully seeking God's direction for sensitivity in daily relationships. It is asking God to open blinded eyes and deaf ears to the call of the gospel. Friendship evangelism means that both personal prayer and the relational dimension are important if people are to come to know Jesus Christ.

Friendship Evangelism — Lessons from a Fishing Trip

There is an interesting story in Luke 5 in which Jesus illustrates several additional relational evangelism principles as he taught his disciples to become "fishers of men."

When Jesus talked about fishing he was not talking about angling with a line and a single hook. He was talking about net fishing. In Jesus' day, people fished on the Sea of Galilee with nets. Fishing was done at night. According to Josephus there were as many as 200 boats out on that lake on a given evening. Each had a torch in the front of the boat so they could see each other and avoid accidents. The story in Luke 5 indicates they had fished all night and caught nothing, when Jesus came and told them to cast their nets on the other side. There are three valuable applications of friendship evangelism principles one can glean from this fishing expedition.

James and John worked as partners in the fishing trade. They were also partners with another boat. Usually there were two persons in each boat and two boats worked in tandem with one another. James and John were in one boat, Peter and Andrew were in another.

Friendship evangelism will be the enterprise of partners. Both

Jesus and Paul reminded their disciples that one sows, another waters; but God gives the increase (John 4:34-38; 1 Cor. 3:5-9). Evangelism is normally the enterprise of partners. Friendship evangelism means we enlist other people in the church to help in the befriending and discipling process. Other people need exposure to the witness of a large circle of Christians.

A second observation is that net fishing is done for a livelihood, while angling is done for sport. This means that evangelism and disciple making are the very life of the church. The church that is not bringing in first generation Christians on a regular basis is a church that already has in it the seeds of death. Churches must be continually reaching. Emil Brunner has said, "The church exists by mission as fire exists by burning."

A third distinction between net fishing and angling is that the former is for keeping and the latter is for catching. Angling is often for sport, for show, for a good picture and an even greater story. Then the fish is thrown back into the water or given away. In net fishing the fish are kept, cleaned and sold. It is the livelihood of the fisherman.

One implication for evangelism is that we call for more than intellectual assent and decisions. Our ultimate concern is the making of disciples. Our burden is the making of responsible members of the Church of Jesus Christ.

It is clear that Jesus' ministry was primarily relational. He shared the Gospel of the Kingdom with the masses but he did so with the personal touch. He repeatedly focused on individuals and smaller groups in his ministry focus. The impact of this approach was far reaching. For example, after his death and resurrection 120 of those people were together in a small room praying. On the Day of Pentecost the 120 (which doesn't sound like very many after three years of ministry) became 3,000 in one day. The 3,000 soon became 5,000. Suddenly Luke no longer uses the word "added" but begins to use the word "multiplied" because the church in Acts was growing so rapidly.

In 1853 a young man named Edward Kimble moved to Boston to work for his uncle in a shoe store. He began attending a church and Sunday School. Kimble had health problems and learned one day that he probably had only a short time to live. In his final months he committed himself to helping his Sunday School class members find Jesus Christ. One day Kimble led a young man to the

Lord in the back room of his uncle's store. This man was D. L. Moody, who became a great church leader and evangelist.

Some years later when Moody recounted his conversion story in England, a pastor named Frederick Brotherton Meyer was hardly impressed. However, a Sunday School teacher heard the same story and when she had shared it with her class of girls, she came back to pastor Meyer all excited. She said, "I told that story about Edward Kimble to my class of girls and I believe everyone of them have given their hearts to the Lord." That simply revolutionized the pastor's ministry. He became better known as F. B. Meyer, internationally known Christian preacher and a leader of the Keswick movement.

Once when F. B. Meyer was in Northfield, Massachusetts he challenged a group of young men with the words, "If you aren't willing to give your all to Christ, are you willing to be made willing?" One young man responded and became a great evangelist in his own right – J. Wilber Chapman. Later on he became moderator of the Presbyterian Church and so he gave up his evangelistic ministry. He gave up that ministry to a young man he had first met as a clerk in the Y.M.C.A. – Billy Sunday.

Several years later in Charlotte, North Carolina, a group of concerned businessmen invited Billy Sunday to conduct a series of preaching meetings. Renewed vitality resulted, so they decided to have a series of meetings every year. Six years later they invited Mordecai Hamm to come and preach at the meetings. While he was preaching three young men in the audience came under conviction. Three days later in one of the meetings they committed their lives to Christ. Their names: Grady Wilson, Cliff Barrows and Billy Graham.

Where did this story begin? With one Sunday School teacher who took his sphere of influence seriously. It illustrates the impact of focusing one's attention on reaching specific individuals with the gospel. It is the most effective long range strategy of reaching the world.

To take Jesus seriously in evangelism is not only to be concerned about his message but also his methods. The principles of relational warmth, availability, call to commitment, involvement, prayer, partnership, reaching new people and disciplemaking which Jesus modeled with his disciples, must continue to be a priority in churches of the Third Way. The practical implications of these principles are numerous. In the book, *The Introvert's Guide to Spontaneous Witnessing*, Selwyn Hughes identifies seven relational skills that impact effective witness: 1) Be yourself, 2) Accept people as they are, 3) Don't try to do people good—love them, 4) Ask the right questions, 5) Learn and remember a person's name, 6) Cultivate openness and transparency, and 7) Pay people compliments.[2] It has been said that one's most effective witness is with persons with whom one has the deepest relationships. The challenge facing every believer is to focus those persons in the circle of ones' family, neighborhood and job and to share in a caring way the meaning of personal faith in Jesus Christ.

Questions and Ideas for Discussion

1. What are the greatest obstacles you have to overcome in friendship evangelism?

2. Discuss the practical implications of the metaphors the Bible uses to describe a Christian as a carrier of good news.

3. The chapter lists five important lessons from Jesus life that relate to friendship evangelism. What are some additional lessons?

4. List the people with whom you have a primary relationship in terms of family members, colleagues at work and neighbors. What specific steps can you take to clarify the good news to these people?

5. If evangelism is a partnership venture, how can other Christians in the church help you clarify the good news in these three relational categories of family, work and neighbors?

6. Share some personal examples of the long range impact of friendship evangelism which brought families and several generations to Jesus Christ.

Peace, Evangelism and
Social Justice in the Third Way

Donald Jacobs

The subject of how peace, evangelism and social justice inter-
face is vitally important for churches of the Third Way. My
perspective on the topic of this chapter has been influenced, to
some degree, by my experience as a missionary in East Africa. I was
there when massive popular upheavals took place as African nations, one after the other, became independent. I was part of that
exhilarating chapter in modern history. My present convictions
were largely formed during that time when I pondered the Scriptures in light of the realities of international inequalities and human
hope.

One cannot address the interrelationship of peace, evangelism
and social justice in the context of Kingdom priorities without some
definitions. To begin, evangelism is revealing Jesus Christ to people. This happens by word of mouth, by deeds of love, and by the
living witness of the Jesus-centered fellowships. All three com-
ponents are essential to healthy evangelism regardless of the
cultural context.

And what is the Kingdom of God? The Kingdom of God exists
where people freely and gladly acknowledge Jesus Christ as their
Savior and Lord. It is entered by the grace of God, and it is
characterized by the reign of God's eternal love. All of those in this
Kingdom are adopted children, according to Ephesians 1:5. They
were once alienated from one another and from God because of
their sin, but now as new creatures in Christ they are bound
together by God's love, which knows no limits.

God's purpose from the foundation of the earth—the reason
for creation itself—is the appearance of these fellowships of God's
love around the world (Eph. 2:15). We see them come into existence today in a variety of circumstances, and we say, Amen.
These fellowships are both the culmination of God's mighty acts in

Jesus Christ, and they are significant appearances of the new creation, the Kingdom of God, in the midst of an age still subservient to the devil.

And what is peace? Paul's statement in the Ephesian letter about the nature of God's peace should leave no one in doubt.

> But now in Christ Jesus you who once were far away have been brought near through the blood of Christ. For he himself is our peace, who has made the two one and has destroyed the barrier, the dividing wall of hostility, by abolishing in his flesh the law with its commandments and regulations. His purpose was to create in himself one new man out of the two, thus making peace, and in this one body to reconcile both of them to God through the cross, by which he put to death their hostility. He came and preached peace to you who were far away and peace to those who were near. For through him we both have access to the Father by one Spirit.
>
> (Ephesians 2:13-18 NIV)

The Theology of Christian Peace

Paul startles us with the words, "Jesus Christ is our peace." That is Kingdom language. Peace is not a gift of Christ; it is not a "product" of the Gospel. Jesus is our peace. If we have Jesus, we have peace. If we have sugar, we have sweetness; if, that is, we eat it.

What does that mean? "We were far away from God, dead," Paul wrote, "in transgressions and sins" (Eph. 2:1). We were enemies of one another (2:14). Then, how are we to be brought into a love relationship with one another? Through Jesus Christ who took on a body, a body which, like the veil in the temple, symbolized the estrangement that existed between God and mankind. That veil represented sin. Sin is our persistence in taking our own way rather than God's way. That veil which separates mankind from God symbolizes our sin, our guilt, our alienation, and our rebellious spirit. Jesus Christ who knew no sin became sin for us. He absorbed all of our sin into that body, into that veil, so to speak; and then he offered his body, that veil, to be broken. He became the sacrifice offered once and forever for man's sin. The veil was rent—the body was broken (Ephesians 2:16).

Since Christ's unique death and resurrection, people who desire full restored fellowship with God enter his holy presence one at a time through that rent veil, the broken body of Jesus Christ (Ephesians 2:19). Not only is fellowship with God marvelously restored, but as the converted ones enter into his marvelous grace they discover that other persons have also entered into Christ. Furthermore, they are amazed that they love the other disciples, and are loved by them. They stand in holy awe and confess, "Indeed, Jesus is our peace."

The reason for "un-peace" in the world is the persistence of sin. The problem is, our desires lead us to please self, not God, that is the essence of sin. According to the Gospel, there is only one way to stand before God free from sin, and that is to stand in Christ, clothed by his right living, gladly accepting Jesus Christ as our sacrifice for sin. We experience the peace of God because the Prince of Peace lives within us seeking to please the Father in all things (Romans 15:3).

This is the bedrock of the New Testament and Anabaptist understanding of God's marvelous peace. Peace is not to be obtained by the sword, nor by forceful coercion. With peace in their hearts, the followers of the Lamb have always placed their welfare in the hand of him who alone can save. The Calvary way means taking up one's cross to follow Christ (Matthew 16:24). As a sheep before the shearer, He opened not his mouth (Isaiah 53:7). The way of the cross for Jesus is the way of the cross for us. This is the authentic base for our persistent refusal to bear arms or to use other coercive methods. To do so would be diametrically opposed to the new understandings, the new values which we experience in Christ. He who lives within us by faith *is* our peace. We are *at* peace, therefore we can exhibit peace.

In the Sermon on the Mount (Matthew 5–7), Jesus spelled out for his disciples how they would live when he would become the sacrifice for sin and then take up residence in their hearts through the power of the Holy Spirit. In that great sermon he did not establish a new law which would also be impossible to obey and produced only guilt and frustration. Rather, it is a description of how people who have entered into the Kingdom of God will act. Embedded in that sermon is the nonresistance ethic of Jesus which is strikingly clear and forceful. But it is not really possible for a person to determine to live that way and thereby please God. We live that life only because Jesus, the Lamb of God, lives within us.

Peace as a Human Longing

The dream of universal peace has tantalized and warmed the human heart for years. The Peace of Rome, for example, was a noble concept. Jesus lived during the "Pax Romana" when the empire was largely at peace, except for the occasional skirmish with the Jews in Palestine. But that great empire crumbled eventually.

Alexander, three centuries before Christ, had a vision for world peace based on Greek culture; but it, too, was short lived. Genghis Khan and Rasha Krishna were visionaries from the East with similar dreams. Universal peace has been sought through universalistic philosophies, through mighty, invincible military legions, through structures and constitutions and covenants. History records their rise and fall in monotonous predictability. Even though we applaud these efforts to obtain universal peace as representing the most noble aspirations of mankind, we know that they all fail for one very simple reason: they do not deal with human sin. Jesus said it right, "There will be wars and rumors of wars." As long as people manufacture peace without reference to the Prince of Peace, they will surely fail in the end; the depressing story of hostility, war and oppression goes on like a tale of desperation. There will be bright spots now and again as well meaning people put together strategies for peace. But peace outside of Christ is temporary at best.

The peace which marks the people of the Kingdom of God operates at several levels. First, we have peace with God through the sacrificial work of Jesus Christ (2 Thess. 3:16). Because of Jesus' self-giving life, we enter into fellowship with God as though we never said "no" to him. We draw near with confidence. Jesus is our Peace with God.

Second, we have peace with "self." Sin, guilt, and self-accusation are all taken away. Even the conscience can be cleansed so that we look at ourselves like God does, through the cross of Jesus Christ (Heb. 10:22).

Third, we have peace with fellow disciples. This begins with spouses, children, people in Sunday School classes, the deacons, church families, and Christians of other persuasions. Fourth, we have peace with neighbors. We live blameless among neighbors because we repent and forgive. We do not retaliate. We refuse to go to war against them. And fifth, we are concerned about peace among those who do not yet believe. Blessed are those followers of Jesus who are hard at work making peace, even among the "nations." God prefers even temporary peace to slaughter and anger. And where hostility disrupts the feeding of people, it is especially harmful.

It is impossible to state categorically how peacemaking is to be done beyond the household of faith. We will not all see eye-to-eye on how to go about confronting the major social evils of our time. But we must have charity one for the other. We should allow for a variety of approaches depending upon gifting, vantage point, etc.

It is also important to remember that there are many signs of God's grace in all cultures of the world, even those cultures in which Jesus is not yet known. But that does not mean that the Kingdom of God is present there. The Kingdom of God appears when people freely acknowledge Christ as Savior and Lord. The Philippian letter makes that clear — "every knee shall bow and every tongue confess" (Phil. 2:10). We do well to avoid the pitfall of universalizing the Kingdom of God by seeing it anywhere that people have compassion on one another.

Evangelism and Concern for Social Justice

The Christian church's commitment to social justice has strong evangelistic appeal. This concern for social justice will find its primary expression in the fellowship of God's people, the church. Justice will be seen most clearly at the congregational level where the peace of Christ reigns supreme, where the brothers and sisters love one another. The Body functions in peace. The very presence of the local Body which includes a variety of persons interacting in peace is one of the most compelling signs of the Kingdom. The same love binds different cultures and nationalities together within one denomination.

As we Anabaptists become more and more culturally pluralistic, we have a new challenge to live at peace as a community which surrounds the planet. Our life together raises questions such as, "How much access does any section of the church have to the resources of the entire brotherhood?" This is one of the pressing questions facing our denomination today. If present growth trends continue, within five years there will be more Mennonites and Brethren in Christ in Africa than in the United States. There will be more in Zaire than in all of Canada. A brotherhood which exhibits its peaceable nature by sharing its resources and by dispersing its power among its less powerful has profound evangelistic appeal. Secondly, Christians must be concerned about aspects of the societies in which they live which are contrary to the spirit of Jesus Christ. Every society faces demonic forces which threaten its very life. Christians do what they can to resist those anti-Godly forces among the general population. How this should best be done is open for discussion, but Christians cannot simply sit back and allow hostility to escalate in society if they have any way at all to do something about it. The brotherhood should allow for several Christlike methods for dealing with these issues.

Christians who follow the Lamb of God are concerned about the welfare of all people. This has powerful evangelistic appeal. It, too, is a sign of the new Kingdom of the Lamb. But we must realize that the Kingdom of God does not come about through legislation or national policies, but by the elevation of Jesus Christ as Savior and Lord.

Cautions Regarding Social Justice

It is at this point, while risking the dangers of generalizing, I feel compelled to state a few affirmations. First, structures do not sin; people do. Structures cannot repent; people repent. Structures cannot be redeemed; people are redeemed. It is doubtful whether Paul had socio-economic structures in mind when he talked about the principalities and powers in the Ephesian, Roman and Philippian letters. In those letters I believe he was referring to the hierarchies of evil spirits arrayed against God's "hosts," his armies. There is a devil, and there are evil spirits. Our battle is not against flesh and blood but against these demonic spirits which pervade our "air." Governments, institutions, homes, trade and economics, all the generic "structures," that is, are in themselves neither good nor evil. It is what people do with those structures which honors or dishonors God. For example, government is neutral but when people use government to perpetuate a cruel institution like slavery or legalized racism as in an Apartheid system, then we are faced with evil. Christians are not anarchists. I am not advocating a passive stance to injustice; evil must be confronted whenever it demonstrates itself. However, it does mean that remedial measures must begin behind the structures and move beyond them. Structural change seldom guarantees ongoing justice. There will always be enough evil people around to corrupt any structure, no matter how "good" it promises to be.

Secondly, popular utopias come and go. Each has some redemptive aspect. The independence movement in Africa was one. Classless socialism was another. The rule of the proletariat was another, a world free of American power and influence was yet another, and a world where every nation has a multi-party democracy is yet another. We must remind ourselves that every utopia was dreamed up on earth. We do well to be very judicious about how much energy we should expend on bringing any of them into existence, or on destroying any of them. A Christian soldier husbands his energies to fight the crucial battles which have not only temporal but eternal consequences. He will not dissipate his strength on peripheral battles.

And finally, all utopias must be tested by the Cross of Jesus Christ. Only Christian eschatology is rooted in the cross of Jesus Christ. From the vantage point of the cross of Christ we are enabled to live in suffering, in the veil of tears, with faith, with hope, and with love. All of the current utopias should be examined in light of the cross, the Second Coming and the promised reign of Jesus Christ.

Practical Directives for Peace-Making Evangelists

The struggle for an integrated theology and lifestyle never comes easily because training and modeling tends to make Christians categorical. It is peace *or* evangelism. It is social justice *or* the proclamation of Good News. It is social concern *or* the Gospel. Jesus calls people of the Third Way away from such a dichotomized "either-or approach" to a "both-and" stance. He calls his disciples to be peace-making evangelists, which has several practical implications. First, it means Christians must refuse a world view which pits the soul against the body. Jesus did not rank the relative importance of word and deed; his disciples should not either. Jesus viewed people as whole beings with all parts interrelated. He also saw them as social beings. Jesus had no sympathy whatsoever for any kind of Platonism or gnosticism. He rejected the Pharisees who disparaged the body as they purified their souls through works. Christians should be as clear on this as Jesus was.

Jesus also rejected the worldview of the Sadducees. They denied the existence of miracles, the resurrection, angels and demons (Mark 12:18). Jesus believed in them all and lived his life in that light. A popular notion which states that Jesus reluctantly accepted a spiritual worldview in order to accommodate his message to the "superstitious" people of his age is wrong. Jesus had the Sadducees' worldview option available to him, and he rejected it out of hand. He put a searching question to the scribes (who were Hellenistic in outlook) in Mark 2:6: "Which is easier, to say your sins be forgiven you or to rise up and walk?" We marvel at the question. The implication of the scribes' protest was that it was harder to forgive sins than to heal the body. Jesus died one death, he sent one Comforter; God packed into Jesus Christ all of his own fullness and makes that available to us for our entire redemption and sanctification (Col. 2:3). All of Christ's work was for all of mankind's needs. There was not one sacrifice for the body, another for the soul.

We do well to repair the damage in our own thinking which resulted from so-called Western "enlightened" education. For two decades I lived among African people who had never divided their world. They could see interconnections which amazed me. Their wholistic perspective made a lot of sense in the light of Jesus' teaching.

Secondly, Jesus Christ needs to be lifted up as the answer to mankind's deep longing for peace. The angels still sing, "Glory to God in the highest, and peace on earth among men who will the good."

Thirdly, Christians need to begin their peacemaking evangelism at home. If Jesus is not bringing peace there, what are we doing proclaiming peace to the world? If we want to move the universe toward the eschaton, one way to do so is to love our spouses. Another is to model sensitivity, care, conflict resolution and the way of peace in the local congregation.

The interrelations between peace and the Good News should also be evident in church relationships. We are asked to live at peace within the denomination and among the denominations. Our ministry is to heal the body of Christ. We are to seek peace with all people and between all people. Let the Spirit of the Lord guide the various Christian fellowships to give authentic local and universal expression to their newfound peace in Christ.

People of the Third Way have a unique place in God's plan because they are vessels chosen to bring men and women to the cross of Christ; they repent and call people to repentance. As repentant, Jesus-loving disciples, they enter into the family of God where they live in peace with one another. They are the Kingdom of God on the earth. They hasten the day of the Lord's return when sin will be destroyed and the devil and his hosts will be utterly cast out. They are in the most sacred vocation the human mind can imagine.

Questions and Ideas for Discussion

1. You may have heard someone say, "Preach Christ, not peace." What do you think that person had in mind? What do you think?

2. Will social justice bring peace? How does peace come? How important is repentance in peacemaking?

3. What is the difference between the Biblical Kingdom of God and a superior political system on the earth?

4. Why do nations rise and fall? Is God at work in their rise and fall? How? For what purpose?

5. Can a person have peace with God and not with fellow Christians?

6. What will make local evangelism more effective in your community?

11

Urban Vision in the Third Way

Christine Michael

The topic of urban evangelism is crucial. The reality around us, whether we like it or not, is that the world is becoming increasingly urban. Seventy-five to eighty percent of the United States population now lives in urban areas. Worldwide, urbanization is occurring so fast that by the year 2000, there will be more persons living in cities of the world than there was total world population in 1965.

The dilemma becomes obvious. The world around us is becoming increasingly urban yet we still think of ourselves as rural denominations. And quite frankly, our track record in the city has not been good. We have few successful urban ministries to which to point.

Perhaps the rural orientation of our history needs to be tempered with some reflection on the meaning of the city in Scripture and a look at the model of evangelism delineated in the book of Acts.

In Scripture there are over 1,400 references to the city of Old and New Testaments. Some of those references speak of the city in negative terms — as a place of worldliness and sin. Other Scriptures, however, speak of the city as the image of the coming Kingdom of God. God's Kingdom is pictured in the New Testament as a city — the New Jerusalem. In many passages, especially in Hebrews and Revelation, the city is the image of hope!

As we look at the book of Acts, it is clear the growth of the early church followed the contours of the urbanized Roman Empire. The disciples intentionally moved into the hearts of cities to tell the good news. They went to the markets, synagogues, and busy streets of cities like Corinth, Philippi, Ephesus, and Rome. The gospel was born in the city of Jerusalem and exploded in growth throughout a chain of cities across the Roman Empire. Consequently, all of the New Testament Churches we know of existed within cities. Until the fourth century, the Christian Church was almost exclusively urban.

Much of the history of our denominations has been a rural heritage—but today we are called to a New Testament model of sharing the good news in the cities. Cities are strategic. People are concentrated there. So are power and decision-making. Communication networks flow from cities. If we are going to be faithful to Jesus' commission to go into all the world, we must learn to be faithful and effective in the city.

Why haven't we been more effective in the city? And what will we need to learn to be more faithful and effective in the next century? Let me suggest three things.

How Do We View the City?

First, if we expect to reach urban people, we must come to appreciate and love the city. As long as we continue to look down our noses, fear, or mistrust it, we will never be effective. We may as well stay out in the rural lands with less than 25 percent of the population. Until we can love the city, celebrate its joys and weep genuinely for its pains, as Jesus wept over the city of Jerusalem, we have no business there. We must come to understand the city as a part of God's creation and blessing. The writer of Genesis tells us that God created the whole world, that God loves and cares for all persons whether rural or urban. If we are to be incarnations of God's love, we, too, will need to learn to genuinely love all of the world, and all persons.

After the Fall of Jerusalem in 587 B.C. and many of the leaders of the Jewish people had been carried off into Babylonian Exile, the prophet Jeremiah wrote a strange thing to those exiles in the city of Babylonia. He said to them, "Seek the welfare of the city, for in its welfare, you will find your welfare." Isn't Jeremiah's advice to the Babylonian Exiles appropos for us today? They were called to infuse the city with shalom—not to form a community apart from the city. Only as we seek the well-being and shalom of the city, will we experience shalom and well-being in our own lives.

In loving the city, we will have to learn to make it our home. I know people in my home congregation who have worked in the city for 30 to 40 years, but still refer to Turkey Run or Clear Creek as "home." When they retire, they move back to those places. They never deeply invest themselves in the city and its welfare. They never really make it their home.

A part of learning to appreciate and understand the city is to learn about urban structures and systems — to be involved in the city, to learn the different cultures that are a part of it. Another way of saying that is illustrated by a story I heard told by George Webber, president of New York Theological Seminary who is active in the East Harlem Protestant Parish. A mouse was being chased vigorously by a cat down a city street. The cat was closing in on the mouse rapidly when suddenly the mouse saw a manhole cover with a tiny opening, just large enough for the mouse to slip down to safety. The mouse waited in the hole for a while, catching its breath. Soon it heard the sound of a dog barking nearby. Certain that the dog had now chased the cat away, the mouse ambled out into the sunlight, only to be grabbed up by the waiting cat. Quickly he realized that there had been no dog; the bark had come from the ingenious cat, who said to the mouse, "In order to survive in this city, you gotta be bilingual."

In order to be effective in the city, we will have to learn to be bilingual. We will need to speak not only the language of faith, but also the language of the city and its people. We will need to understand and be involved with the city, love and appreciate it, if we want to share the good news there in the twenty-first century.

Can We Link "Faith and Works?"

The second mandate if we are to be faithful and effective in the city is that we must link together our "faith and works." Our evangelism must be a wholistic evangelism that addresses the needs of the whole person — physically, emotionally, economically, and spiritually. We have been good about caring for individuals. Faithful evangelism in the city will have to be as concerned about the structures that hurt people as it is about individuals themselves. In order to do this, we must rethink the dualism of what is sacred and what is secular. In the past, we have conveniently labeled things like unemployment, housing problems, welfare lines as "secular," meaning that then the church had no responsibility for those. Instead we would confine ourselves to what we labeled "sacred" — worship services, Bible studies, and passing out tracts. God's demand for justice, which permeates the Old and New

Testaments, must radically broaden our understanding of sacred. A paper on world hunger says, "My bread is a material concern. My brother and sister's bread is a spiritual one."

When Jesus announced his ministry in the synagogue at Nazareth, he said it would be to "preach good news to the poor, to proclaim release to the captives, recovery of sight to the blind, to set at liberty those who are oppressed, to proclaim the acceptable year of the Lord." If we are to call persons to follow Jesus Christ as Lord, can our ministry be any less than this? To be unwilling to involve ourselves in the deep hurts and injustices of the city, is a denial of Incarnation.

Until three months ago when I took my present position, I pastored a congregation in Indianapolis for seven years. The Northview Church building is located in a neighborhood that experienced white flight about 12 years ago. In less than a year the neighborhood went from 100 percent white to about 50 percent white, 50 percent black. It was a chaotic, turbulent time in which the churches of the area were paralyzed by their own fear.

When I arrived in 1978, the black-white tensions had lowered and a modicum of stability had been restored. However, banks were still "red-lining" (refusing to make home mortgage loans) to the area. Over half of the businesses had moved out of the neighborhood shopping plaza. The absentee owner of the center refused to do any of the much-needed maintenance and vandalism was rampant. The few places left to shop, a grocery and hardware, were threatening to move soon.

What does it mean to preach good news to a neighborhood like that? Was there any way for Northview to be an incarnation of Jesus Christ without addressing that most obvious need in the neighborhood? We struggled together to realize finally that economic development wasn't just "secular,"—it was "sacred." The economic health of the neighborhood, the real estate values, the ability of blacks and whites to live and work together—all of those things were a part of God's concern. They were indeed sacred because they were critical issues in the lives of people for whom Christ died. If we at Northview were going to witness to the life-changing love of Jesus Christ, it would have to include rolling up our sleeves and working for justice in our community, before any one would take us seriously. To make a long story short, after five long years of work, the New York real estate company, who was using the shopping center as a tax write-off, was finally bought out by a 50-50 joint venture between the neighborhood association and a local developer. The renovated center is now bustling with store owners and shoppers again, the crime rate is down. Home mortgage loans can be secured again. It stands as a model that blacks and whites together in our neighborhood association could work together. It is a symbol, I think, of the Kingdom of God we read about in Revelation, made up of people of different colors and races and cultures who all praise God's name. The Incarnation happens in strange and unexpected ways—stables in Bethlehem, grocery stores and a hardware in an integrated neighborhood struggling for survival. When will we learn to see God present in the nitty-gritty stuff of life? When will we learn to cease our artificial dichotomies of sacred and secular? When will we learn to blend our faith and works? Only then will we be faithful and effective in the city.

Do We Love and Care About People?

A third criteria for urban evangelism is that we share our faith out of a love and concern for other persons—not simply in order that we survive or be successful. In Luke 9 Jesus tells his disciples that whoever seeks to save his own life will lose it but whoever loses their life for his sake will find it. Only when we are willing to lose our lives as a church will we find life.

One of my favorite Old Testament stories is the 2 Kings account of four lepers perishing with hunger outside the walls of the city of Samaria. The city was suffering under siege by the Syrians, and so no one in the city had any food. They knew that if they simply stayed where they were, they would starve to death. The worst the Syrians could do would be to kill them, so they decided to surrender to their enemies and beg for mercy. However, when they reached the Syrian camp, they found that God had caused them to hear the sound of a great army and that the enemy troops had fled and left behind an abundance of food! The four lepers feasted and made merry! They enjoyed their good fortune until finally the realization dawned on them that they were selfishly hoarding these blessings, while others in their city were starving to death. They said to one another, 'This is the day of good news! Let us go and share it with others!'

We, too, have been given good news to share with others. We share that good news, not to save our own life, but so that others might have life — have life in all of its abundance.

To summarize my hunches about urban evangelism in the twenty-first century:

1. We must learn to genuinely love the city in a way that we have not done in the past.

2. We must let go of the false dichotomy of "sacred and secular," and radically broaden our definition of sacred. We must blend together faith and works.

3. We must share our faith because of our love for persons — not to insure our own survival or success. We must be willing to lose our life in order to find it.

George MacLeod wrote: "I simply argue that the cross be raised again at the center of the marketplace as well as on the steeple of the church. I am recovering the claim that Jesus was not crucified in a cathedral between two candles, but on a cross between two thieves; on the town garbage heap; at a crossroad so cosmopolitan that they had to write his title in Hebrew and in Latin, and in Greek . . . at the kind of place where cynics talk smut, and thieves cursed and soldiers gambled. Because that is where he died. And that is what he died about. And that is where church people ought to be and what church people ought to be about."

Go! Go into all the world! Into the inner and private spaces of human life . . . into the spheres of public policies. Go into all the world and preach the good news to the rich and to the poor. To the powerful and the powerless, to the majority and the minorities, in Chicago, in Fresno, in Philadelphia, in Winnipeg and to the ends of the earth says the Lord of the Church!

Questions and Ideas for Discussion

1. The author of the chapter points out three reasons why Anabaptists have not been effective in the city. What other reasons can you think of?

2. It is easy to think of the negative aspects of the city (i.e. violence, crime, poverty, crowding etc.), what are the positive

aspects of the city?

3. In what specific ways can your congregation link "faith and works"?

4. George MacLeod's quote talks about what "church people ought to be about." In your own words, what do you think church people ought to be doing?

12

Urban Evangelism Strategies in the Third Way

Henry J. Schmidt

It was the nineteenth century evangelist, Dwight L. Moody, who said that cities are the mountain peaks of society. Everything runs downhill from the city; therefore, if we are to reach the nation for Christ we must "strategize" for the cities. The gospel must penetrate the city if it is really to penetrate American society, for the city is the soul of society. Cities determine the destinies of nations. They are centers of communication, influence, cultural life, government, finances and education. The challenge of urban specialist Roger Greenway that "he who wins the city, wins the world,"[1] must be taken with greater seriousness by Mennonite and Brethren churches as we face Century 21.

Two sociological realities today significantly affect evangelization, namely, the urbanization of the world and the internationalization of cities. According to the Population Reference Bureau the world which was 28 percent urban and 72 percent rural in 1950, became 41 percent urban and 59 percent rural by 1975. In 1985 the global population is approximately 50 percent urban and the projections are that by 2000 the ratio will be 55 percent urban and 45 percent rural. What is almost overwhelming is the rate of growth and the development of a large number of mega-cities. For example there are now 240 World Class cities (population of 1 million or more). That figure will become 500 cities by the year 2000. By the year 2000 there will be 58 cities of over five million people compared with 29 today. Half of the urban growth will come from natural increase, the rest from people escaping the poverty in the countryside. In the year 2000 the biggest cities of the world will be: Mexico City—31 million; Sao Paulo—26 million; Tokyo-Yokohama—24 million; Shanghai and New York-N.E. New Jersey—23 million; Beijing—20 million; Rio de Janeiro—19 million; Bombay, Calcutta and Jakarta—17 million.[2] Put simply the world net growth produces two Chicagos every month (one of which is Asian). Or to make it more concrete for North Americans, Mexico City, now with a population of 18 million, is growing at a rate of 6.2 percent per year (80,000 a month or one million a year), meaning that two San Franciscos a year are produced within Mexico City alone.[3]

If the predictions are true that by the year 2000 at least 3.2 billion people will live in urban areas, then strategizing to reach these diversified peoples today must become the church's highest priority. Urban sociologists remind us that one of the chief characteristics of the city is its international flavor. Major cities become the entry point for new immigrant groups. The Western church, which tends to be white, Anglo-saxon, middle class, Protestant, needs to be reminded of the fact that in 1985 only 20 percent of the world's population is white and by 2025 this figure is expected to drop to 10 percent. Will the church seriously wrestle with the implications of urbanization and internationalization in its evangelism strategy?

Strategizing has to do with the implementation of a mission vision. It does not refer to some standardized plan that is applied unilaterally, but to a means of communicating the good news in contextually appropriate ways to different peoples. For example, how does the church reach the seven million people of Chicago, where ethnicity is the order of the day? Or where the largest population of Poles resides outside of Warsaw? Or where more than one million Hispanics reside? Or where the black population comprises almost one-third of the city's population? Strategizing for Chicago and all cities must address four major issues: churches in transition; reaching ethnic groups; developing specific target groups; and church planting.

Churches in Transition

Probably the most unchanging characteristic of large cities is constant change. Grady Clay in his remarkable book, *Close-up*, says it well: "Cities, in short, are forever rewriting their repertoires."[4] After visiting scores of cities all across North America, Clay concludes that the real continuity is that cities are "forever changing." Landmarks change, neighborhoods change, politicians change, businesses change, and the people of the city change. How can the urban church be established and thrive in the face of such flux? In contrast with urban churches, rural churches offer the security of limited turnover of people and minimal community transition. In the cities, we must plan and plant the Gospel with an understanding that transition will be a natural part of church life.

Whether the change that faces people in cities comes through population growth or decline, redevelopment, shifts in racial compositions of urban populations or greater variations in lifestyles, the church must be constantly reading the needs of its constituency. To not do so is to become reactive, irrelevant and defensive rather than being pro-active, flexible and visionary.

In describing typologies of communities within urban areas, it is helpful to think in terms of five distinct types: downtown district, inner city, stable community, suburbs, and rural-urban fringe. These five types may also be described sociologically as one of three categories: pre-transitional, transitional and post-transitional. Since churches either exist or will need to be started in all areas of the city, an awareness of demographic data is imperative for good planning. Since communities change, the church must design its message, program and activities to address the persons within the community and city. Since by nature the city is dynamic rather than static, churches cannot avoid change by simply relocating from downtown and inner city to the stable community or suburbs, because change is an integral part of those areas of the city as well. In a most helpful article on "Attitudes and Urban Transition," Craig Ellison challenges the church to find its security in an unchanging God and to be more flexible in how we do church in the city. He says: "Our ministries will be ineffective if we cherish our racial-ethnic composition, our order of worship, our meeting schedules, our style of music and preaching more than we love those who need the Saviour but are kept out of the Kingdom because we are unwilling to make changes that would draw them to Christ."[5]

In focusing the arrival of immigrant ethnic groups, Time magazine called the Los Angeles area "The New Ellis Island." Students in the Los Angeles Unified School District speak 104 languages. The Albert Einstein Medical Center in Philadelphia is staffed to service patients in 28 languages. These serve as sample illustrations of the multi-ethnic character of cities, with distinct neighborhoods, ethnic and language communities. While earlier waves of immigrants were primarily white Europeans who settled in growing cities and found jobs as craftsmen, factory workers and merchants, the past two decades have made American cities more diverse and colorful. We can't talk about America as a melting pot anymore. It is more like a salad bowl or a stew pot, in which every ingredient preserves its own distinct flavor. Cities are the focal point of an ethnic mix that includes Latin Americans, Asians, and Middle Easterners. While English will remain the predominant language, other cultures and languages will find their place. This means that Christian workers who function in a multi-cultural society will have to acquire a second language and be equipped for cross cultural ministry.

Mission strategist Donald McGavran speaks of the urgency of "making disciples of all nations" (*ta ethne*—different people groups and population segments).[6] The urgency of ministry to the millions of immigrants to new lands is rooted in two major concerns. One is the fact that when people are uprooted and experience cultural upheaval they are more open to the gospel. A second is a need to reach first generation migrants in their primary language since they cannot be as readily absorbed into existing churches because of the language barrier. Although the shape and style of ethnic churches will vary greatly, depending on where language groups are in the cultural assimilation process, the church must demonstrate vision for and acceptance of ethnic people with their language and culture. The targeting of the vast number of international students studying in American universities may in fact be one of our best mission strategies for bringing the Gospel to all the nations.

Most Protestant congregations are made up of English-speaking, middle-class people. The prominent form of urban church is the neighborhood church. In the past, urban neighborhoods have formed along social class lines, racial and ethnic uniformity. So the urban church has developed as a reflection of its neighborhood homogeneity. In the past several decades urban neighborhoods have given way with increasing rapidity to change caused both by the suburbanization of racial and ethnic groups and the "gentrification" of the urban core. More typically today the context of the urban congregation is one of pluralism and diversity. This means the church must rethink its strategy of evangelization.

If, in fact, one of the major shifts in moving from a rural to urban psyche is a change from primary, face-to-face relationships to secondary, more indirect relationships, the church has to think in terms of target groups. While people in apartments, high rises, condominiums or in single family dwellings may not necessarily know their neighbors, this does not mean they do not have personal relationships. They find them in other channels. In *The Sociology of the City,* Spates and Macionis write: "What seems to be significant about the urban environment is not the lack of ties of attachment, but how these seem to vary. That is, cities seem to encourage alternative types of relationships more than other environments do."[7] There are all sorts of urban voluntary associations that people belong to ranging from film societies, singles' bars, health and natural food centers, fitness centers, recreation clubs, neighborhood watch programs and consciousness-raising groups of all kinds. The challenge facing the church is to target the different relational networks of urban people in the areas of professions, politics, kinship, volunteer associations and ethnic groups. In the midst of the pluralism the urban church needs to ask, "Who is there in the city besides middle-class family units?"

In strategizing various target groups in the city it is striking to note that most mainline evangelical churches are missing the same three groups in terms of effective evangelism; the poor, the multi-housing dwellers and the young, urban professionals.

The Neglected Poor

Often the poorer section of the city is occupied by various ethnic groups and is referred to as the inner city, the low-income community or the ghetto. It is often the sector of the city in which there is much government activity and control but little activity by the private sector. It is the other side of the American fence, opposite the side where the grass is green. The poor are frequently left behind without the gospel witness, as churches abandoned the inner city for suburbia and upward social mobility. This does not mean there is not a need for churches in the suburbs, but if Christ died for all people, the church must work with greater intentionality at planting churches in all segments of the city.

A second neglected group in the city are those who live in multi-family housing units such as high rise apartments, condominiums, government housing projects and penthouses. For example, in Dallas, Texas 56 percent of the population lives in multi-family housing; in Houston the percentage is 51. Apartment dwellers are notoriously hard to reach. Some people live in apartments for social and economic reasons, but others chose apartments because they want to be left alone.

With the projections that multi-family housing will continue to increase drastically during the next two decades, one of the key questions that faces the church is how to reach the isolated people living in apartment housing. One of the key problems is accessibility to these highly populated living structures. Another concern is a strategy to create a greater sense of community among the apartment dwellers as an entry point for building the church. For example, the Village Apartment complex in Dallas has 7,000 multi-family units in one complex. They have sought to deal with the need for community by providing recreation as a network for relationships; they have 32 softball teams, an Olympic-size pool, plus 37 other pools.

Since not all apartment buildings are alike and attract different clientele, each type requires somewhat of a unique evangelistic church. The dearth of literature on ministry to apartment people is its own commentary on the church's lack of strategizing to reach this population segment.

The Neglected Young Urban Professionals

A third neglected population group by most mainline churches are the people in their mid-20s to early 40s. These people are referred to as the baby boomers (born between 1946 and 1964). They comprise roughly one-third of the population and include the much-publicized "yuppies" (young upwardly mobile urban professionals). Between 1980 and 1990 the number of Americans who are 25 to 45 years old will increase by 30 percent.[8] Besides being more highly educated and affluent than their predecessors, they represent the first generation to be raised on television and to have grown up under the threat of nuclear war. They are the generation that Carl Dudley describes as having "belief without belonging," that is, they claim to have a personal faith but do not relate to the mainline institutional church.[9] Larry McSwain notes that the loss of membership and religious participation in mainline denominations can be accounted for by persons who were born between 1940-1960 and has subsequently led to the "greying of the church."[10] While the median age in the United States has changed from 26 years of age in the mid-60s to 31 in 1980, one half of all "born again" evangelicals live in the South and 45 percent are age 50 or older.

The implications are clear. We have a nontraditional, highly educated, young and middle adult group loosely connected to the church in which the leaders over forty share values with young people (due to the conservative shift in culture to the right). This group feels outside the institution because of a different value orientation. It is a group that has experienced more at an earlier age than any previous generation. It does not accept simple answers to complex problems. It is for the most part a group that marries later, has fewer children at a later age and divorces more frequently. It is the generation that has heard the traditional message of the church, gone to Sunday School, prayed in school, saluted the flag and attended summer camp, but for many the social ferment of the 1960s with civil rights, Vietnam, the new morality of sexual promiscuity, and theological pluralism was too much of a battering. The baby boomers will not be reached by a traditional church with its stereotyped programs.

This group represents the greatest potential for leadership and church ministry during the next several decades but they will have to be reached and recruited by the church as a first step. They are full of promise because most live in the city as business and professional people. They have an urban psyche and are the church's greatest resource in reaching the city.

Planting New Churches

Church planting is the most effective evangelistic methodology. There is not a denomination in North America today that is growing that is not planting new churches. The reasons for this are not difficult to discern. New churches start with a clear vision and commitment to the mission of reaching people. Such vision and commitment is contagious also for established congregations who have prayer, personnel and financial commitment to a new work. In some cases established churches have sent a substantial core of members to be a part of the new work, which in turn created more space and incentive for outreach within the sending church.

Secondly, there is strong statistical evidence that the ratio of conversions per member is higher among new churches and congregations that are less than five years old than among more established churches. Thirdly, new churches often reach population segments that are not being ministered to by existing churches. There is an excitement about being part of something new and shaping its direction. Furthermore, new churches have fewer established patterns and hence can be more creative, flexible and mobile in how they do church. In terms of evangelism strategy this means that an appropriate goal for urban mission is that a living church be planted within easy distance and in the culture of every person in the city.

Churches of the Third Way must commit themselves to the priority of urban evangelism in Century 21. John Naisbitt's *Megatrends* has volumes to say to the church in terms of trends that affect both our vision and strategy for reaching the city.[11] Particularly the trends towards decentralization, shifting population to the Sun Belt, high tech-high touch, participatory democracy and multiple options call for new vision and evangelism strategy. Unlike most sociological analysis, Naisbitt ends his book in an upbeat mood, "My God, what a day to be alive."[12] The question is, can the church be upbeat about urban evangelism in Century 21? Do God's words "I have many people in the city" stir us with a vision for the multitudes in the exploding metropolises so we say, "What a God-given opportunity?" Will we respond to the challenge and live in the city, not in fear but with the compassion of Christ, to see not only the masses, but individuals and particular people groups who are like "sheep without a shepherd?" Will we respond in obedience to a vision for evangelizing every people group in the city with a commitment that says, "Whatever it takes to bring them the gospel, I will pay the price?" May history record our vision, strategy and commitment to urban evangelism in Century 21 in the words of Rupert Brooks, "May God be thanked who matched us for this hour."

Questions and Ideas for Discussion

1. How do you respond to the massive urbanization of the world? How do your feelings affect your vision and commitment to urban mission?

2. What transition have you had to face as a local church? How can your church help urban churches that need to refocus their vision and program because of transition?

3. What particular unreached people groups are there in your local community? What would it take to begin a ministry among one or several of these groups?

4. The author of the chapter identified three neglected groups of people among most evangelical churches (the poor, the yuppies and apartment dwellers). What changes would have to take place in your local church to effectively minister to one or several of these neglected groups?

5. Who are the new people that have been added to your church in the past two years and how were they reached? What does this tell you about strategies for reaching the unchurched?

13

Multiplying Churches in the Third Way

Don Yoder

In *Planting Churches Cross-Culturally*, David J. Hesselgrave states, "The primary mission of the Church, and therefore, of churches is to proclaim the gospel of Christ and gather believers into local churches where they can be built up in the faith and made effective in service, thereby planting new congregations throughout the world."[1] The church is not an afterthought in the plan of God. When Jesus ministered on earth he prophesied that he would build his church and the gates of Hell would not overpower it (Matt. 16:16-18). He gave himself in death that the church might be born and grow (Eph. 5:25). His work continues from Heaven as he sanctifies or "calls out" the church and prepares it for its final presentation (Eph. 5:26-27). It was the church that Jesus commissioned to "Go into all the world and preach the gospel and make disciples of all nations" (Matt. 28:19-20).

The New Testament is clear about the interrelationship between gospel proclamation and the establishment of churches. Paul's commitment to preach the gospel resulted in the establishment of numerous congregations. His New Testament letters are addressed to churches, and highlight the prominent place of the church both as base for healthy spiritual nurture and for dynamic witness.

Churches of the Third Way continue to place a high priority on the multiplication of churches. The purpose of this chapter is to address the importance of planting new churches from three perspectives: basic reasons for multiplying new churches; basic ingredients for effective church planting; some basic models for multiplying churches.

Basic Reasons for Multiplying New Churches

We must first ask, "Do we not have enough churches already?

(250,000 in North America). Is not our real problem the competition between churches? What we need is not more churches, but better churches, more cooperation and more unity." There are at least six answers to these honest questions about the need for churches of the Third Way to prioritize the multiplication of new congregations.

Paul was the greatest church planter who ever lived. According to Roger Greenway, Paul's strategy of evangelism can be outlined in three steps: 1) The conversion of sinners; 2) The establishment of churches: 3) Witnessing to Christ's lordship in society and the world. The Gospel, as the leaven of the Kingdom, entered society through the changed lives of converted people and the churches which they composed.[2] Paul's strategy for mission was from converts to churches, from churches to the city as a whole, and from the city to the entire known world.

In his own ministry of church planting Paul observed, "I planted, Apollos watered but God gives the increase" (1 Cor. 3:6). It is important in church planting to remember that it is God who gives the increase. That increase is, of course, related to our faith, anticipation and belief that God "is not willing that any should perish" and "that he will build his church." However, when we move into an area, it is essential to do so with attitudes of obedience and expectation. We are starting new churches because it is God's will. We expect him to honor the faithful proclamation of the gospel and to bring a congregation of believers together.

Lyle Schaller reports that the most important argument for new church development is that this is the most effective means for reaching unchurched persons.[3] Numerous studies have shown that 60 to 80 percent of the new adult members of new congregations are persons who were not actively involved in the life of any worshiping congregation immediately prior to joining that new mission. By contrast, most long-established churches draw the majority of their new adult members from persons who transfer in from other congregations. New Christians as well as young adults (born since 1940) are found in disproportionately larger numbers in new missions than in the older churches.

There are certain sociological factors that keep a church from growing (e.g., crowded facilities, insufficient parking, not enough group life, etc.). Planting a new church is a marvelous strategy for evangelistic outreach. For example, if 50 to 80 people leave one congregation to plant another church, something significant happens in both churches. The new church has a large enough core to begin significant ministries. Within a year the sending church will grow and replace those who left.

Churches of the Third Way have had a strong relational emphasis, which may have been counterproductive, in terms of church planting. We like to be together and know each other and it has therefore been difficult to give our blessing to a group who left to start a new church. Too often our attitudes toward people leaving our churches on such ventures have been those of loss rather than of commissioning or sending people in mission.

While motivation for church planting must be more than survival, it is a fact that denominations and churches that are not reaching new people will eventually die. It is estimated that 30 percent of the world population is Christian, and perhaps one-fourth of those are committed Christians. This means there are millions of people who need to be reached with the gospel, and thousands of new churches needed if we are to fulfill the Great Commission.

I have personally been involved in several church planting ventures in the Phoenix-Tempe area. When we first moved to the Tempe area I counted all of the churches in the Tempe/Mesa/Chandler Yellow Pages. I took the population of those three cities and divided it by the number of churches and the results were shocking. If everybody in those cities would have awakened on Sunday morning and decided to go to church there would have been more than 2,000 people in every available facility. There was an urgent need for more churches in that area.

Church planting is a stimulus and encouragement to other existing congregations. It helps to revitalize other churches in the denomination by making them partners in evangelistic ministries.

New churches should not be a threat but an encouragement because they usually attract a different clientele due to their particular style and focus. This means that new churches represent additional help in gathering the ripened harvest and in expanding Christ's Kingdom.

A fifth reason for multiplying congregations is leadership development. When a group is commissioned to start a new congregation, it often includes key leaders from the sending congregation. What happens? New people with leadership gifts move into the leadership position in that congregation. The leadership gifts of

those who are a part of this new congregation are also discerned
and utilized. When congregations don't start new churches, a
generation of leaders is often overlooked and undeveloped. A basic
problem in established churches is that leadership tenure tends to
be too long and there is not enough emphasis on developing new
leaders.

A final reason for multiplying congregation is that it is the
most effective means of reaching the diverse people groups in the
city. The church must constantly guard against viewing the city as a
uniform mass of people who can be reached with a monolithic
strategy. There are "different strokes for different folks" when it
comes to churches. The kinds of churches that appeal to suburban
folk will not work in the inner city. It is important that suburban
churches be multiplied because that is where the greatest concentra-
tions of people are located. However, we cannot neglect a wholistic
strategy which includes inner-city churches. This will take careful
planning, cooperative suburban-urban coalitions and a mutual support system. It means churches must be open to a different style of
church, different criteria for evaluating success, and a different
system of lay and pastoral training. The point is that every people
group and every area of the city ought to have a clear gospel witness
and a vibrant local fellowship.

Basic Requirements for Multiplying Congregations

While it is beyond the scope of this chapter to discuss the different models for church planting, there are five basic
characteristics that are applicable to all new church starts. These include: a church planter, a core of church people, a philosophy of
ministry, thorough demographic research, and an understanding of
unchurched people.

Multiplying congregations requires a church planter or a team.
Whether a team or an individual is called as a church planting
pastor, directional, effective leadership is very important. Too
often we have gathered a group of people together as a nucleus
without giving careful attention to leadership. The end result has
been a lot of good fellowship but very little planning and strategizing to penetrate the community.

A recent study conducted by the Fuller Institute for Evangelism and Church Growth focused on the characteristics of a

church planting pastor. The study was funded and supported by 11 denominations (which included the Mennonite and Mennonite Brethren Conferences). Each denomination furnished a list of church planting pastors who were interviewed personally or by telephone to develop a church planter's profile. While the study indicated 45 desirable traits, it highlighted 11 primary characteristics desirable for church planters. These included: ability to build body consciousness, faith, vision, commitment to growth, personal motivation, responsiveness to the community, utilization of gifts, expertise in creating ownership of ministry, ability to build relationships, flexibility and family support in ministry.[4] The church planting pastor sets the tone, style and direction for a new congregation in a way that is not necessarily the case in established churches.

The second requirement for church planting is some Christian people, unless one is starting a pioneer work. Lyle Schaller suggests that 80 to 100 people is a good beginning nucleus. A nucleus of this size has the advantage of providing sufficient social networks for support, adequate people and financial resources for ministries and is large enough to overcome the barriers that normally face a small church (under 50). Fuller Evangelical Association suggests a nucleus of 50. It does make a difference whether one begins a worship service with seven people or if one begins with a larger group that has been built up through visitation, outreach ministries and advertising. The smaller the group starts the greater its tendency to remain small for a longer period of time.

In my opinion, it is definitely advantageous for a new congregation to begin with a healthy nucleus and the blessing of one or several established congregations. It boosts the morale, develops greater accountability, establishes a support system, and encourages a new church in its mission. Without an adequate support system, church planting can be a very lonely experience, not only for the pastor but for leaders who have left established churches and friendship ties to become a part of this new mission.

A third essential to healthy congregational multiplication is a philosophy of ministry. It is important to know the kind of church that is being planted. Is the philosophy of ministry geared to reaching unchurched people or is its primary concern the gathering of Christians? Is the emphasis a fortress church or a ministering body?

A philosophy of ministry has to do with the priorities and strategies of a particular church. The philosophy of ministry must include a specific focus for reaching people in the community. Whether the specific strategy is single parent families, unwed mothers, street people, young families, or young urban professionals, the point is the church exists to minister to people. When that commitment to ministry has been spelled out and owned by the church, the style and appropriate strategy for the particular group can be determined.

Jesus ministered to the needy and the broken people in society. The church should do no less. At times the task and emotional drain may be overwhelming, but the ministry perspective must be kept in focus. This is why it is important to share the ministry burden with a group of elders or leaders and to have the support of sending churches.

Thorough demographic research helps a new church determine its clientele and strategy of evangelism. How does one research a community? There are a number of helpful resources such as the Census Bureau, Chamber of Commerce, social service agencies, public utilities, public school systems and churches. It is helpful not only to evaluate statistical data but to interview key individuals in city planning commissions, neighborhood services and local pastors. This can help to determine community needs and discern which needs and people groups are being overlooked.

A final essential ingredient for starting new churches is a deep sensitivity and commitment to unchurched people. Rick Warren of the Saddleback Valley Community Church in Laguna Hills, California says that "reaching the unchurched is not an option for new churches — it's a matter of survival!" The spiritual dynamics of prayer, Bible study and obedience to the Holy Spirit heighten sensitivity to the unchurched.

Furthermore, in church planting we need to learn to think like the unbeliever. This means we must have contact and exposure with non-Christian friends. Contact with non-Christians must be a priority in new church planting. It is sad but true that the longer people are in the church, the fewer non-Christian friends we tend to have. Without significant relationships with the unchurched we cannot learn to think like they think, and to understand their hurts and perspectives.

Our witness to the unchurched needs to focus on their felt

needs. There is a sense in which the community must set the agenda for the church. It is too easy for churches to assume we know the needs and to place our agendas on the unchurched. A preferable strategy is to ask questions, and let them articulate needs. Those needs may relate to coping with stress, child rearing techniques, conflict resolution, marriage communication, financial management or cardiopulmonary resuscitation classes. The church can then respond with a positive strategy that addresses the felt needs of people.

Models of Congregational Multiplication

It has been said that "a picture is worth a thousand words." One of the best ways to learn both the priority and technique of multiplying congregations is to look at particular church models that have been effective. The purpose of sharing these live case histories is to focus on a diversity of models and on transferable principles.

Hopewell Mennonite Church—Elverson, Pennsylvania

The Hopewell Mennonite Church was a rural congregation of approximately 60 people until 10 years ago. For 50 years they ministered primarily to German ethnic families. The church had a ministry to children and to a few families in the community. Ten years ago the congregation split over a theological controversy revolving around the ministry of the Holy Spirit. One group left to start another church. The remaining handful at Hopewell called Merle Stoltzfus to pastor the church.

During the past 10 years God has performed a miracle with the Hopewell congregation. In the first year after the division, the Lord brought an influx of new people into the church. Internal differences subsided and congregational relationships began to heal. Today the Hopewell Mennonite Church has an attendance of 800 people. It has been instrumental in starting nine new congregations, which includes an additional 1,200 people.

In a workshop, Stoltzfus shared four key principles of how an established, dying church was revitalized and became a catalyst for planting new congregations.[5] First, leaders must promote a vision. The pastor and church leaders have to start putting seeds of visions into people's minds. "In five years this church is going to be full and we will have to enlarge our facilities." Even though no one in the church believed it or could see it, somebody had to start talking vision. A leader has to start talking about an idea a year or two ahead of time so the congregation can break it in and become growth oriented.

A second factor is a workable plan of evangelism. The type of plan people use is not important; what is crucial is that Christians are equipped to lead a person to Christ in a step-by-step procedure. The bottleneck in many churches is that Christians are told to lead people to personal commitment to Jesus Christ, but they have never been shown how to help a person make a decision. "Whenever I have a chance to lead people to Christ publicly in a church service, I see that as an opportunity to teach Christian people how to lead non-Christians to commitment. Wherever possible I take individuals with me when I visit people so they can see and hear me share the gospel."

A third significant key to the growth at the Hopewell church is the development of lay leaders. The church has a large number of small groups whose primary function is prayer, sharing and caring. Small group leaders function as elders. If a person has enough initiative to take hold of a small group, to lead it, and to disciple people, he can develop his eldership and leadership abilities. The best way to get a person ready for leadership is to have him lead a small group. He has to study. He has to prepare a lesson every week, he has to know how to lead people to the Lord, he has to learn how to minister to people, how to pray for them when they're sick, how to visit them when they're in the hospital. He's really becoming a pastor at that point.

The way the church can overcome the bottleneck of not having sufficient trained pastors is to train its own. Of the nine daughter congregations, seven are today pastored by leaders who have been trained in the local congregation. They have been called out of the congregation and discipled by the pastor and other elders.

A fourth factor that has affected the growth at Hopewell is the healthy emphasis on worship. At a typical Sunday service, the first half is spent in singing. Singing usually includes Psalms sung, choruses, and musical groups, which encourages the participation of young people. This is followed by a testimony or two from new converts or people who have had a significant spiritual experience.

Often people will listen to the testimony when they won't listen to preaching. The sermon is usually brief and is outlined on an overhead projector. At the end of the sermon people are encouraged to come to the front to make a commitment and to share a message they have heard from the Lord. The service usually lasts one and a quarter hours. It is dynamic, encouraging and invigorating to the people who come.

Santa Clara Ethnic Chinese Mennonite Church — California

Adam and Jeanette Liu and their four sons moved to Santa Clara, California from Taiwan in early 1981. They are part of a large number of Southeast Asian refugees who have resettled in the "Silicon Valley" and have found employment in the computer industries. Adam had served as a pastor and conference leader with the fellowship of Mennonite Churches in Taiwan for a number of years. The Liu's were sensitive to the Holy Spirit and soon began a Bible Study in their home with ethnic Chinese refugees from Cambodia. The Bible studies grew and on the Sunday following Thanksgiving in 1981, a new church was born as the Santa Clara Ethnic Chinese Mennonite Church. Today 80 to 100 people are a part of this congregation which meets each Sunday afternoon. A year and half ago a second congregation was started among Southeast Asians in the South Bay area. Most of the 45 members of this second congregation are from Taiwan and one half of them are high school students.

Pastor Liu has three observations on church planting among new arrivals. First, new arrivals are an open field for evangelism because they face so many major adjustments to a new culture. While most new arrivals come to North America with high hopes of fulfilling their educational and vocational dreams, the initial hurdles seem overwhelming. In addition to culture shock and language problems, new arrivals are often anxious about finding a job, securing adequate housing, passing a driving test, meeting eligibility requirements for employment, applying for public aid and finding medical help. They feel isolated from the rest of society because they are "strangers in a new land." Liu noted that they have led most of the people to Jesus Christ through their response to the practical, adjustment needs or new arrivals. Liu said, "The urban church is not just an ivory tower, concerned about attendance, offering and activities, but it is a lighthouse shining in the darkness to care for the wanderers, the oppressed, the abandoned and the poor. Mennonites who have a heritage of being a wandering people and caring for the poor can have a powerful ministry in the city among new arrivals."[6]

Second, church planting among new arrivals means that the congregation consists primarily of first generation Christians. While this is cause for rejoicing because people have turned "to God from idols" (1 Thess. 1:9), it causes some unique struggles. One is the lack of knowledge regarding God, the nature of the church and congregational responsibilities and obligations. There is a great need for foundational, Biblical teaching. Another struggle is to integrate their new faith with daily life. The temptation to go back to their old ways is strong. The matter of letting faith in Jesus Christ influence economic values, education objectives, family relationships, and vocational goals is an ongoing struggle. A third concern that first generation Christian congregations face is the need for leaders and positive role models. Paul faced the same problems in his ministry in establishing new churches in Asia minor, so it is not unique to these two Southeast Asian congregations. The training of leaders must be a priority because the church in a pagan environment must have some "footprints" to follow. Paul's emphasis on the qualities of leaders in Titus 2 and 1 Tim. 3 is clearly related to his concern that first generation Christians have positive models to emulate.

A third concern in ethnic urban church planting relates to facilities. Liu admits that church is not first of all buildings, but people; but he believes that if a congregation is to progress and move toward maturity it must find a place to call "home." The Santa Clara Ethnic Chinese Mennonite Church has moved its worship place three times in the past four years. Currently they meet on Sunday afternoon in the Mennonite Brethren facilities of the El Camino Bible Church. While any urban congregation must be flexible in its structures and programming, it is difficult to build with continuity without a permanent place. For long range development, Liu says "we need our own church building."

Laurelglen Bible Church — Bakersfield, California

The Laurelglen Bible Church had a unique beginning in January, 1978 when 80 people from three Mennonite Brethren families in the Bakersfield-Shafter, California area formed the nucleus of this new congregation. After a three-month interim with church planter Elmo Warkentin, the congregation called Ed Boschman to pastor the church. Since April, 1978 the congregation has grown from 82 charter members and a Sunday morning attendance of 100 to a membership of 391 and an average attendance of 540 during 1984-85. Today the church has two morning worship services, a pastoral staff of three and an active interest in helping start another congregation in southeast Bakersfield.

In reflecting on their attempt "to be a twentieth century church, rooted in first century biblical principles," Boschman prioritized five areas which have helped to shape the present congregation.[7] First, a clear focus on the church's purpose and ministry model from Acts 2:42. The philosophy of ministry is captured in four words: 1) Celebrating — worship together; 2) Loving — sharing, relationships, mutual support; 3) Becoming — teaching, lay ministry mobilization; and 4) Communicating — outreach-evangelism. Undergirding these according to Boschman, "prayer has been the single most significant factor that has impacted our philosophy of ministry. We have been committed to prayer in men's groups, women's groups, discipling groups, couple's groups and Bible Study groups." Prayer has helped keep mission at the center of Laurelglen. The church has focused on the local body of Christ as a "mission — a soul hospital where those who are saved need constant care." Boschman says, "I remind the church frequently that our purpose is not to get comfortable, but to stay current in our relationship with the Lord, to grow to maturity on him, and to bring people to Jesus Christ." In their church publicity and practice they have not majored on "Mennonite Brethren" because they are concerned about reaching the community and about initial barriers that any denominational name carries. People who are a part of the congregation today have told Boschman that they would not have initially visited the church had it been called Mennonite Brethren. At Laurelglen the emphasis is on the centrality of a living, shared faith. They spend a lot of time and energy doing that, as is evidenced by the influx of new people who are reached primarily through the network of friendships.

Second, Laurelglen has sought to contextualize the gospel by being "all things to all men" (1 Cor. 9:16), within doctrinal bounds.

In its middle class suburban community, the church constructed appropriate facilities for its "people group." There is an openness to new people. Services have the air of informality with dignity. The church has a formal visitation plan (modification of James Kennedy's Evangelism Explosion), but normally visits only the "warm contacts," by pre-arranged appointments in teams of two. In emphasizing contextualization, Boschman stressed the importance of flexibility. "We have bent sideways, frontwards and backwards to resist concretization and institutionalization as a developing congregation."

A third priority is an open, visionary leadership model. "It is important not only to lead with vision, but to lead openly and confessionally. People must have occasion to give their "input" and evaluation if they are to own the vision. The leadership style at Laurelglen is "inspirational and instructional—not dictatorial." Leadership has sought to provide a strong mission vision to the church by budgeting and planning for outreach ministries.

Fourth, a meaningful, informed membership is priority at Laurelglen. Every person who joins the church must participate in six membership classes. The classes deal with local church identity and identification with Mennonite Brethren, history, theology, vision (local and global) and mutual expectation of members and the church as a body. Boschman reports two normal responses in these on-going six week sessions: one is that a number of persons have been converted through the class instruction. Secondly, they have had some attrition as a result of their "high demand" on involvement and accountability. "Some people say 'this is not for me' and therefore they do not join and some of them do not continue to attend."

A final emphasis at Laurelglen has been a high level of lay ministry involvement. Pastoral leadership is in the church to "equip others to do the ministry —*with* them, but not *for* them." One implication of such a philosophy is that leadership has to make provision for additional equippers as a body grows. Laurelglen added a second pastor when the membership was 220 and the annual attendance average was 360. A third staff person was recruited when the membership was 331 and the attendance 436. The addition of a fourth pastoral staff person is projected when the membership is 500 and the attendance 680. The church's priority on equipping and mobilization in lay ministry is evidenced by the fact that seven out of every 10 adults are actively involved in some task or role. "A ministering people is a celebrating, growing, reproducing and aspiring people," Boschman said. "People need to be helped to sharpen their ministry skills, which is our major task as pastors, and then encouraged and inspired to invest them for the Lord."

There is no substitute for the church and no other organization can take its place or do its work in the world today. The church is of God; it came from God and not by man. The church of our Lord Jesus Christ was brought into existence to fulfill the Great Commission to make disciples of all nations. The local church in each community is the basic agency on earth for the ministry of the Gospel in that community. The local church is an expression of the body of Christ to its community and God's agent for evangelism and ministry. The primary mission of the church as it relates to the world is to be a witness in every community of the grace of God and to plant churches which will multiply themselves and extend the witness of our Lord. This can best be fulfilled by planting new churches in every community that become new expressions of God's love and grace in that community.

Questions and Ideas for Discussion

1. How valid is Paul's strategy for mission as outlined by Roger Greenway for the 21st century church?

2. Why is new church development — church planting an effective means of reaching new people?

3. List and discuss the six reasons given for new churches. What are some additional reasons for starting new congregations.

4. What basic requirements for starting a new church would you add to the five listed in the chapter?

5. What characteristics in the life of your church would be a hindrance to starting a new church? What characteristics would be supportive of a new church start?

6. What important lessons did you glean from the three church planting models given in this chapter?

NOTES

Chapter 4. Covenant Community

1. C. S. Lewis, *Surprised by Joy: The Shape of My Early Life,* (New York: Harcourt, Brace and Company, 1955) 20-21.
2. James Dunn, *Baptism in the Holy Spirit* (Naperville, IL: A. R. Allenson, 1970), 73-78.
3. Henri J. Nouwen, *Reaching Out: The Three Movements of the Spiritual Life* (Garden City, NY: Doubleday, 1975), 46-54.
4. *Ibid.*, 51.
5. John Naisbitt, *Megatrends: Ten New Directions Transforming Our Lives* (New York: Warner Press, 1982), 52-53.

Chapter 7. The Meaning of Conversion in the Third Way

1. Richard J. Neuhaus, *Freedom for Ministry* (New York: Harper and Row, Publishers, 1979), 8.
2. Alfred C. Krass, *Evangelizing Neopagan North America* (Scottdale, PA: Herald Press, 1982), 53.
3. Marlin Jeschke, "What is the status of children in the believers church?" *Christian Living*, February 1981, 3.
4. Paul Loffler, "Conversion to God and His Kingdom," London, 1966 (Mimeographed), 4.
5. *Ibid.*, 10.
6. John Regehrin, *Conversion: Doorway to Discipleship*, ed., Henry J. Schmidt, (Hillsboro KS: Board of Christian Literature of the Conference of Mennonite Brethren Churches, 1980), 58.
7. Marlin Jeschke, *Believers Baptism for Children of the Church* (Scottdale, PA: Herald Press, 1983). The summarizing diagram on p. 122 is helpful in making the distinction.
8. *Ibid.*, 120.
9. *Ibid.*, 149.
10. Hans Kasdorf, *Christian Conversion in Context* (Scottdale,

PA: Herald Press, 1980), 79.

11. *Ibid.*, 79

12. Gabriel Fackre, *Word in Deed* (Grand Rapids, MI: Wm. B. Eerdmans Publishing Company, 1975), 84-98.

13. *Ibid.*, 98.

Chapter 8. Discipling New Converts in the Third Way

1. Garth Hunt, "What God Is Doing Around the World." An address at the Billy Graham School of Evangelism, October 15-19, 1984, Vancouver, British Columbia.

2. Henry Noewen, an opening address to the World Council of Churches, July 1983, Vancouver, British Columbia.

3. Robert E. Coleman, *The Master Plan of Evangelism* (Old Tappou, NJ: Revell, 1963), 18.

4. Matthew 5:1; Luke 6:12-16, 10:1.

5. Acts 2:40-42, 12:2; John 20:30-31.

6. As reported by John Wesley White at Billy Graham Crusade workers rally in Vancouver, September 11, 1984.

7. Others might be more comfortable with the following outline given at Alive '85 which, however, is more of the reformed theological traditions.

GOD

Is merciful. He loves you and wants to give fellowship, forgiveness, purpose and heaven to all of us (Luke 12:32).

Is just. He has set up laws that eventually give people what they deserve. He cannot allow sin and disharmony (Proverbs 14:12).

WE

Are made in the image of God but become sinners who lack trust and bring disharmony (Romans 3:23).

Cannot save ourselves. God's gifts cannot be earned or deserved (Ephesians 2:8, 9).

CHRIST

Is God. He is history's unique prophet, priest and King (Luke 3:22).

Paid for our sin and offers us God's free gifts of life (Romans 6:23).

WE NEED

To surrender as much of our sinful, divided selves as we can to as much of Jesus as we can understand (1 John 1:9).

To become disciplined in letting Christ live in and through us (Romans 8:9-11).

8. Samuel Shoemaker, *How to Become a Christian* (New York: Harper and Row, 1953), 71.
9. Allen Stibbs, General Editor, *Search the Scriptures* (London: InterVarsity Fellowship, 1967).
10. Robert D. Foster, "Seven Minutes with God," (Navpress, Box 6000, Colorado Springs: Colorado 80934).
11. Louis H. Evans, Jr., *Covenant to Care*, (Wheaton, IL: Victor Books, 1982), and Elizabeth O'Connor *Call to Commitment* (New York: Harper and Row, 1963), 34.
12. "Let's Face It," available from Faith and Life Audiovisuals, Newton, Kansas.
13. Lyle B. Schaller, *Activating the Passive Church*, (Nashville, TN: Abingdon, 1981), 122ff.
14. Bill Pannell, An address at Regent College, "Evangelism and Social Action," Vancouver, B.C., October 1985.

Chapter 9. Friendship Evangelism
1. Arthur G. McPhee, *Friendship Evangelism* (Grand Rapids, MI: Zondervan Publishing House), 1978); Wayne McDill, *Making Friends for Christ* (Nashville: TN: Broadman Press, 1979); Rebecca Manley Pippert, *Out of the Salt-Shaker and Into the World* (Downer's Grove, IL: InterVarsity Press, 1979); Joe Aldrich, *Lifestyle Evangelism* (Portland, OR: Multnomah Press, 1981); Jim Peterson, *Evangelism as a Lifestyle* (Colorado Springs: Navpress, 1980).
2. Selwyn Hughes, *The Introvert's Guide to Spontaneous Witnessing* (Minneapolis, MN: Bethany Publishing House, 1983), 66-82.

Chapter 12. Urban Strategies

1. Roger S. Greenway, *Apostles to the City* (Grand Rapids, MI: Baker Books, 1971), 11.
2. Ray Bakke, "Urban Evangelization: A Lausanne Strategy Since 1980," *International Bulletin of Missionary Research*, 8 (October 1984) 4: 152-154.
3. Ray Bakke, "Strategy for Urban Ministry," *Theological Student Fellowship Bulletin*, Vol. 8 (March-April, 1985): 20.
4. Grady Clay, *Close-up* (New York: Praeger Publishers, 1973), 11.
5. Craig W. Ellison, "Attitudes and Urban Transition," *Urban Misson*, 2 (January 1985) 3: 17.
6. Donald McGavran, "New Urban Faces of the Church," *Urban Mission* Vol. 1, No. 1 (September 1983), 3-11.
7. James L. Spates and John J. Macionis, *The Sociology of Cities* (New York: St Martin's Press, 1982), 48.
8. "America's Middle-Age Spread," *Review Magazine* (March 1985), 35.
9. Carl S. Dudley, *Where Have All the People Gone?* (New York: The Pilgrim Press, 1979), 3-17.
10. Larry L. McSwain, "The Cultural Captivity of the Church," in Larry L. Rose and C. Kirk Hardaway, eds., *The Urban Challenge* (Nashville: Broadman Press, 1982), 55.
11. John Naisbitt, *Megatrends: Ten New Directions Transforming Our Lives* (New York: Warner Books Inc., 1982).
12. *Ibid.*, 252.

Chapter 13. Multiplying Churches

1. David J. Hesselgrave, *Planting Churches Cross-Culturally* (Grand Rapids, MI: Baker Book House, 1980), 20.
2. Roger Greenway, ed., *Apostles to the City* (Grand Rapids, MI: Baker Book House, 1978), 79-87.
3. Lyle E. Schaller, "Why Start New Churches?" *The Circuit Rider*, May 1979, 3.
4. Charles Ridley, "Church Planter Performance Profile," *Pastoral Profiles for Church Planters, A study by the Fuller Evangelistic Association,* January 6-8, 1985, Pasadena, California.
5. Merle Stoltzfus. "Training Congregational Leaders for Evangelistic Growth," Alive '85 Workshop, Denver, Colorado,

April 11-15, 1985.
6. Adam Liu, "The Voice of a Young Urban Church," Santa Clara Ethnic Chinese Mennonite Church, 2582 Elliot Court, Santa Clara, California 95051.
7. Telephone Interview with Ed Boschman, September 12, 1985. Laurelglen Bible Church. 2801 Ashe Road, Bakersfield, California 93309.

RESOURCES FOR FURTHER STUDY

Chapter 1.

Bosch, David. *The Spirituality of the Road*. Scottdale, PA: Herald Press, 1978.

Costas, Orland. *The Integrity of Mission*. New York: Harper and Row, 1979.

Ellul, Jacques. *The Presence of the Kingdom*. New York: Seabury, 1964.

Green, Michael. *Evangelism in the Early Church*. Grand Rapids, MI: Wm. B. Eerdmans Publishing Co., 1970.

Newbigin, Lesslie. *The Open Secret*. Grand Rapids: MI: Wm. B. Eerdmans Publishing Co., 1978.

Trueblood, Elton. *The Future of the Christian*. New York: Harper and Row, 1971.

Walker, Allen. *The Whole Gospel for the Whole World*. Nashville, TN: Abingdon, 1972.

Wallis, Jim. *The Call to Conversion*. New York: Harper and Row, 1981.

Chapter 2.

Best, E. *A Commentary on the First and Second Epistles of the Thessalonians*. London: Adam and Charles Black, 1972.

Bruce, F. F. *1 and 2 Thessalonians*. Waco, TX: Word Book Publishers, 1982.

Marshall, I. H. *1 and 2 Thessalonians*. Grand Rapids, MI: Wm. B. Eerdmans Publishing Co., 1983.

Moore, A. L. *1 and 2 Thessalonians*. Greenwood, SC: The Attic Press, 1969.

Morris, Leon. *The First and Second Epistles to the Thessalonians*. Grand Rapids, MI: Wm. B. Eerdmans Publishing Co., 1959.

Ward, R. A. *Commentary on 1 and 2 Thessalonians*. Waco, TX: Word Book Publishers, 1973.

Chapter 3.

Brown, Raymond E. *The Gospel According to John*. The Anchor Bible, vol. 1 and 2. New York: Doubleday and Co., 1970.

Halverson, Richard C. *How I Changed My Thinking About the Church*. Grand Rapids, MI: Zondervan Publishing House, 1972.

Morris, Leon. *The Gospel According to John*. The New International Commentary of the New Testament. Grand Rapids: MI: Wm. B. Eerdmans Publishing Co., 1971.

Tasker, R.V.G. *The Gospel According to St. John*. Tyndale New Testament Commentaries. Grand Rapids, MI: Eerdmans Publishers, 1960.

Stott, John R. W. *Christian Mission*. Downers Grove, IL: InterVarsity Press, 1975.

Stott, John R. W., ed. *Christ the Liberator*. Downers Grove, IL: InterVarsity Press, 1971.

Chapter 4.

Arias, Mortimer. *Announcing the Reign of God*. Philadelphia, PA: Fortress Press, 1984.

Dunn, James. *Baptism in the Holy Spirit*. Naperville, IL: A. R. Allenson, 1970.

Lewis, C. S. *Surprised by Joy: The Shape of My Early Life*. New York: Harcourt, Brace and Co., 1955.

Naisbitt, John. *Megatrends: Ten New Directions Transforming Our Lives*. New York: Warner Press, 1982.

Nouwen, Henri J. *Reaching Out: The Three Movements of the Spiritual Life*. Garden City, NY: Doubleday, 1975.

Smith, James E. *Friendship Evangelism*. Anderson, IN: Warner Press, 1958.

Sweazey, George E. *The Church as Evangelist*. New York: Harper and Row, 1978.

Chapter 5.

Bubna, Donald L. and Sarah M. Richetts. *Building People Through a Caring Fellowship*. Wheaton, IL: Tyndale House, 1978.

Cook, Jerry and Stan Baldwin. *Love, Acceptance and Forgiveness*. Glendale: Regal Books, 1972.

Havlik, John F. *People-Centered Evangelism*. Nashville, TN:

Broadman Press, 1972.

Neighbour, Ralph. *The Seven Last Words of the Church*. Grand Rapids, MI: Zondervan Publishing House, 1973.

Synder, Howard A. *Liberating The Church*. Downers Grove, IL: InterVarsity Press, 1983.

Tillapaugh, Frank. *The Church Unleashed*. Glendale: Regal Books, 1982.

White, Jerry. *The Church and the Parachurch*. Portland, OR: Multnomah Press, 1983.

Womack, David. *The Pyramid Principle of Church Growth*. Minneapolis, MN: Bethany Fellowship Inc., 1977.

Chapter 6.

Brunk, George R., ed. *Encounter with the Holy Spirit*. Scottdale, PA: Herald Press, 1972.

Carter, Charles W. *The Person and Ministry of the Holy Spirit*. Grand Rapids, MI: Baker Book House, 1974.

Graham, Billy. *The Holy Spirit*. Waco, TX: Word Book Publishers, 1978.

Green, Michael. *I Believe in the Holy Spirit*. Grand Rapids, MI: Wm. B. Eerdmans Publishing Co., 1975.

Marshall, Catherine, *The Helper*. Waco, TX: Chosen Books, 1978.

Neighbour, Ralph W. *The Touch of the Spirit*. Nashville, TN: Broadman Press, 1972.

Wood, A. Skevington. *Life by the Spirit*. Grand Rapids, MI: Zondervan Publishing House, 1963.

Chapter 7.

Baillie, John. *Invitation to Pilgrimage*. Grand Rapids, MI: Baker Book House, 1976.

Barclay, William. *Turning to God*. London: Epworth Press, 1963.

Fackre, Gabriel. *Word in Deed*. Grand Rapids, MI: Wm. B. Eerdmans Publishing Co., 1975.

Jeschke, Marlin. *Believers Baptism for Children of the Church*. Scottdale, PA: Herald Press, 1983.

Kasdorf, Hans. *Christian Conversion in Context*. Scottdale, PA: Herald Press, 1980.

Krass, Alfred C. *Evangelizing Neopagen North America*. Scottdale, PA: Herald Press, 1982.

Morris, George E. *The Mystery and Meaning of Christian Conver-*

sion. Nashville, TN: The World Methodist Council, 1981

Schmidt, Henry J., ed. *Conversion: Doorway to Discipleship*. Hillsboro, KS: Board of Christian Literature of the Conference of Mennonite Brethren Churches, 1980.

Chapter 8.

Aldrich, Joseph C. *Lifestyle Evangelism*. Portland, OR: Multnomah Press, 1981.

Arn, Win and Charles Arn. *The Master's Plan for Making Disciples*. Pasadena, CA: Church Growth Press, 1982.

Bartel, Floyd. *A New Look At Church Growth*. Newton, KS: Faith and Life Press, 1979.

Coleman, Robert E. *The Master Plan of Evangelism*. Old Tappin, NJ: Revell Press, 1963.

Perkins, John. *With Justice for All*. Ventura, CA: Regal Books, 1982.

Schaller, Lyle E. *Assimilating New Members*. Nashville: TN: Abingdon Press, 1978.

Wagner, Peter. *Leading Your Church to Growth*. Ventura, CA: Regal Books, 1984.

Chapter 9.

Hughes, Selwyn. *The Introvert's Guide to Spontaneous Witnessing*. Minneapolis, MN: Bethany Publishing House, 1983.

Innes, Dick. *I Hate Witnessing*. Ventura, CA: Vision House, 1983.

McDill, Wayne. *Making Friends for Christ*. Nashville: TN: Broadman Press, 1979.

McPhee, Arthur G. *Friendship Evangelism*. Grand Rapids, MI: Zondervan Publishing House, 1978.

Metzger, Will. *Tell the Truth*. Downers Grove, IL: InterVarsity Press, 1981.

Miles, Delos. *How Jesus Won Persons*. Nashville, TN: Broadman Press, 1982.

Peterson, Jim. *Evangelism as a Lifestyle*. Colorado Springs, CO: NavPress, 1980.

Pippert, Rebecca Manley. *Out of the Salt-Shaker and Into the World*. Downers Grove, IL: InterVarsity Press, 1979.

Chapter 10.

Conn, Harvie M. *Evangelism: Doing Justice and Preaching Grace*.

Grand Rapids: MI: Zondervan Publishing House, 1982.

Escobar, Samuel and John Driver. *Christian Mission and Social Justice*. Herald Press, 1978.

Kraus, C. Norman. *The Authentic Witness*. Grand Rapids, MI: Wm. B. Eerdmans Publishing Co., 1979.

Ramseyer, Robert L., ed. *Mission and the Peace Witness*. Scottdale, PA: Herald Press, 1979.

Scott, Waldron. *Bring Forth Justice*. Grand Rapids, MI: Wm. B. Eerdmans Publishing Co., 1980.

Shenk, David W. *Peace and Reconciliation in Africa*. Nairobi, Kenya: Uzima Press, 1983.

Shenk, Wilbert, ed. *Anabaptism and Mission*. Scottdale, PA: Herald Press, 1984.

Chapter 11.

Driggers, Carlisle. *Models of Metropolitan Ministry*. Nashville: TN: Broadman Press, 1979.

Dudley, Carl. *Where Have All Our People Gone?* New York: Pilgrim Press, 1979.

Greenway, Roger. *Apostles to the City*. Grand Rapids, MI: Baker Books, 1978.

Pasquariello, Ron; Donald Shriver; and Alan Geyer. *Redeeming the City*. New York: Pilgrim Press, 1983.

Shriver, Donald and Karl Ostrom. *Is There Hope for the City?* Philadelphia, PA: Westminster Press, 1977.

Chapter 12.

Ellison, Craig. *Saying Goodbye to Loneliness*. New York: Herald Books, 1980.

Greenway, Roger, ed. *Discipling the City*. Grand Rapids, MI: Baker Books, 1979.

Rose, Larry L. and C. Kirk Hadaway, eds. *An Urban World*. Nashville, TN: Broadman Press, 1984.

Rose, Larry L. and C. Kirk Hadaway, eds. *The Urban Challenge*. Nashville, TN: Broadman Press, 1984.

Hopler, Thom. *A World of Difference*. Downers Grove, IL: InterVarsity Press, 1981.

Mitchell, Arnold. *The Nine American Lifestyles*. New York: Warner Books, 1983.

Palen, John J. *The Urban World*. New York: McGraw-Hill Inc., 1981.

Ziegenhals, Walter E. *Urban Churches in Transition*. New York: Pilgrim Press, 1978.

Chapter 13.

Amberson, Talmadge R. *The Birth of Churches*. Nashville: TN: Broadman Press, 1979.

Chaney, Charles L. *Church Planting at the End of the Twentieth Century*. Wheaton, IL: Tyndale House, 1982.

DuBose, Francis M. *How Churches Grow in an Urban World*. Nashville, TN: Broadman Press, 1978.

Greenway, Roger S. *An Urban Strategy for Latin America*. Grand Rapids, MI: Baker Books, 1973.

Hesselgrave, David J. *Planting Churches Cross-Culturally*. Grand Rapids, MI: Baker Books, 1980.

McGavran, Donald. *Understanding Church Growth*. Grand Rapids: MI: Wm. B. Eerdmans Publishing Co., 1970.

Peters, George W. *A Theology of Church Growth*. Grand Rapids, MI: Zondervan Publishing House, 1981.

Womack, David. *Breaking the Stain-Glass Barrier*. New York: Harper and Row, 1973.